Praise for *The Wizard and the Warrior*

"Truly something novel and useful among the current books on contemporary leadership. Bolman and Deal have again created a book that is both a conceptual gem and a handy practical reference. *The Wizard and the Warrior* will make us think carefully again about leadership in general and about our own style in particular."

> —Walter F. Ulmer Jr., lieutenant general, U.S. Army (Ret.),
> former president and CEO, Center for Creative Leadership

"Bolman and Deal's *The Wizard and the Warrior* could be your secret weapon. Read. Learn. Then lead with confidence."

> —Thomas Keller, The French Laundry

"With *The Wizard and the Warrior* Lee Bolman and Terry Deal have followed up the insights of *Reframing Organizations* with a grounded and entertaining set of very useful stories. The numerous examples of historical and contemporary figures and their life stories serve to bring leadership ideas alive in a way that few books achieve. A great and useful read!"

> —Len Schlesinger, vice chairman and chief operating officer, Limited Brands

"Rarely do scholars attempt, let alone succeed, as Bolman and Deal have done so palpably, to encompass the polarities of leadership. They have thrown their arms around the inspirational, on one hand, and the tough, practical, and sometimes brutal, on the other. Through wonderful stories, they convincingly illustrate the real challenges and possibilities of living life grounded by larger purposes and the courage to interrogate reality. Anyone practicing leadership, or dreaming of doing so, should read this book."

> —Ronald A. Heifetz, Center for Public Leadership, John F. Kennedy
> School of Government, Harvard University; author of *Leadership
> Without Easy Answers* and *Leadership on the Line*

"Terry Deal and Lee Bolman have established the 'gold standard' for looking at leadership. In *The Wizard and the Warrior* they show how to integrate the two sides of leadership. It is about fighting the good fight, but not losing sight of the magic—it is about making the word flesh. This is a must-read for anyone who cares about becoming a better leader."

> —Paul D. Houston, executive director, American Association
> of School Administrators

"Warriors and wizards! Crazy metaphors for leaders? No! Compelling insights that Bolman and Deal have distilled from organizational life, illustrating them with fascinating stories. They convinced me that we as leaders can achieve our mission and care for our people more effectively by embracing the reality of combat and magic, of power and spirit, in our organizations. If you're a good leader, this book will make you better."

—Colonel Larry R. Donnithorne, author, *The West Point Way of Leadership: From Learning Principled Leadership to Practicing It*

"I find *The Wizard and the Warrior* a fascinating and enjoyable read. The premise is exactly what it set out to be, a prod and a guide to trumpet the true legacy of leadership. The self-inventory guidelines stimulate an interesting integration of fantasy and myth (through Harry Potter's Dumbledore, Merlin of King Arthur's court, and Tolkein's Gandalf) with the realities of business tycoons such as Oprah Winfrey, Herb Kelleher, and Mary Kay Ash, as well as the political wizardry of U.S. presidents. The book provokes the reader to understand the immeasurable potential of the wizard and warrior in each of us that can create change and challenge."

—John Keola Lake, kumu-in-residence, Chaminade University of Honolulu, Hawai'i, head of Hawaiian traditions

"This book is a must-read for all who are pursuing the journey of leadership. It provides in-depth insight into passion and power, and how they are the very essence of leadership. It will be of great value for all those in leadership positions at J.E. Dunn."

—Terrence P. Dunn, chief executive officer, J.E. Dunn Construction Company

"What do wizards and warriors have to do with good leadership? A lot, it turns out. So hoist your inner sword or wand and let Bolman and Deal instruct you on how to wield it effectively, and on how notable combatants from Joan of Arc to Bill Gates have fared."

—John Alexander, president, Center for Creative Leadership

THE WIZARD AND THE WARRIOR

LEADING WITH PASSION AND POWER

LEE G. BOLMAN
TERRENCE E. DEAL

JOSSEY-BASS
A Wiley Imprint
www.josseybass.com

Published by Jossey-Bass
A Wiley Imprint
989 Market Street, San Francisco, CA 94103-1741   www.josseybass.com

Jossey-Bass books and products are available through most bookstores. To contact
Jossey-Bass directly call our Customer Care Department within the U.S. at
800-956-7739, outside the U.S. at 317-572-3986, or fax 317-572-4002.

Jossey-Bass also publishes its books in a variety of electronic formats. Some content
that appears in print may not be available in electronic books.

Library of Congress Cataloging-in-Publication Data
Bolman, Lee G.
   The wizard and the warrior : leading with passion and power / Lee G. Bolman,
Terrence E. Deal.—1st ed.
        p. cm.
   Includes bibliographical references and index.
   ISBN-13: 978-0-7879-7413-8 (cloth)
   ISBN-10: 0-7879-7413-7 (cloth)
  1.Leadership. 2. Management. I. Deal, Terrence E. II. Title.
   HD57.7.B645 2006
   658.4'092—dc22

                                                           2005036845

Printed in the United States of America
FIRST EDITION
HB Printing   10 9 8 7 6 5 4 3

CONTENTS

THE WIZARD AND THE WARRIOR

For three of the teachers from whom

we have learned so much:

Chris Argyris

James March

John Meyer

PART ONE

CONFRONTING THE WIZARD AND WARRIOR WITHIN

Why a book about wizards and warriors as models for leadership?
Because, as Peter Drucker once said, everything you learned is wrong.
At best, it is misleading and insufficient. You typically learn in school,
workshops, and seminars that if you can manage the work and serve the
people, you have what it takes. It's not true. Maybe you have enough stuff
to be a pretty good manager, but it takes a lot more to be a good leader.

*I*n our earlier book, *Reframing Organizations,* we argued that managers need first to get an accurate reading on situations before taking action. The problem, we found, is that they typically relied on two lenses (we call them frames) when they needed four. The two they use focus on structure and people, and both are important and valuable perspectives. They help you become sensible and humane. But they work best in a rational world populated by reasonable people. No one lives in such an orderly world anymore. Today's organizations are inherently messy and unpredictable.

That's why bad things keep happening to good managers. They get blindsided. Their career gets stunted or goes off the rails. The boss blames them for things that weren't their fault. Someone else gets a promotion that they deserved. A coworker flubs a project but tosses the dead cat into their yard. After a particularly devastating day at the office, one disillusioned manager commented, "I thought I had covered all the bases, and then realized that everyone else was playing football. I had a great strategy for the wrong game."

This happens because managers are running on two cylinders *~ cultural* when they need four. Two other frames—political and symbolic—are required to make sense of the roiling, moving targets that organizations serve up every day. They take us into a world dominated by power and passion. The bad news: that's just where managers are usually weakest. We know this from our research worldwide and across sectors. Inattention to these two ways of thinking and behaving is a debilitating Achilles' heel.[1]

Managers shy away from politics because they see its dynamics as sordid or because conflict scares them. They fear losing control and losing out. They cling to the illusion that if organizations were run right, they wouldn't be political. Most managers have an even harder time grasping the elusive and mysterious influence of symbols. Discounting culture as fuzzy and flaky, they don't see it, even though it's there and influencing everything they do. Great leadership doesn't happen without addressing these political and cultural issues head-on. Leaders cannot afford to stay on the sidelines and play it safe. Someone has to be willing to stand up and put it on the line. That's why we need more wizards and warriors.

Leaders are defined by their legacy, which is shaped over time from hard decisions they must often make—whether to lay off or not, to fight or withdraw, to merge or go it alone, to go against the grain to achieve more or follow the rules but gain less. At such critical choice points, great leaders access the wizard's mastery of the symbols and the warrior's command of power. The wizard role enables them to bring imagination, creativity, meaning, and magic. The warrior role mobilizes strength, courage, and willingness to fight as hard and long as necessary to fulfill their mission.

The wizard and the warrior inhabit two distinct but overlapping worlds. The warrior's world is a place of combat, of allies and antagonists, courage and cowardice, honor and betrayal, strength and weakness. It is sometimes a world of danger and destruction—war really *is* hell. One of the noblest and most enduring human quests is the search for peace, for a way to avoid war's terrible costs. Yet combat and conflict continue to be endemic in human life. A group or organization that has no warriors is at great risk —of being overrun by one that does.

The wizard inhabits a realm of possibility, magic, and mystery. The wizard's strength lies not in arms or physical courage, but in wisdom, foresight, the ability to see below and beyond appearances. The wizard brings unshakable faith that something new and better really is out there. The tools of the wizard's trade are values, icons, ritual, ceremonies, and stories that weave day-to-day details of life together in a meaningful symbolic tapestry. An enterprise without wizards is sterile and often toxic. People are out for themselves rather than bonded together by a shared spirit.

The greatest leaders move in and out of both roles, even if they are more comfortable with one or the other. Or they partner with someone who has talent in a role they find hard to assume. Look, for example, at *Time* magazine's millennial list of the greatest leaders and revolutionaries of the twentieth century.[2] It includes both angels

(Pope John Paul II) and devils (Adolph Hitler). Some, like Margaret
Thatcher and Mao Zedong, were legendary warriors, known for
their steely resolve and zest for combat. But Thatcher and Mao were
both talented wizards as well. Others, such as Mahatma Gandhi and
Nelson Mandela, were best known for near-miraculous impact on
their respective nations, relying more on spiritual than political or military resources. But neither was a stranger to combat. The three U.S.
presidents on *Time's* list—Theodore Roosevelt, Franklin D. Roosevelt,
and Ronald Reagan—all combined the warrior's courage and strength
with the wizard's alluring magic and hot hope.

What is true for world leaders holds for a growing number of
practitioners who have become successful because they have learned
to appreciate these fundamental dimensions of power and passion. An
example is Dr. Jim Hager, a candidate for National Superintendent of
the Year in 2004:

> During the first half of this decade, my focus as a superintendent
> was on improving student learning by concentrating on people and
> structure. I now spend considerable energy and time dealing with
> individuals and narrow interest groups bent on immediate satisfac-
> tion of their parochial needs and wants, regardless of the conse-
> quences for the common good. More time is spent resolving conflicts
> that roil as special interests compete for power and resources. I
> also have to devote time and energy to symbolic issues to ensure
> the essence of public education. Since the current villagers have no
> sense of the village, today's superintendent must use rituals, sto-
> ries, ceremonies and other symbols to transform a splintered culture
> into a common community focus on shared educational values.[3]

It is tragic to subject young people, our hope for a better future,
to the crossfire of special interests and a cacophony of values. We'll
reap the consequences later on. But it's not only our nation's schools

at peril. Hager echoes the observations of many other leaders across the country and around the world. Wise leaders in business, health care, the military, and nonprofit endeavors wrestle with the same vexations. Hager has an advantage—he recognizes the political and symbolic challenges he faces and acts accordingly. Many would-be leaders are less fortunate. They persist in believing that creating a humane and rational workplace is enough for high performance. Year after year they are disappointed when their labors fall short.

Wizard and warrior are roles that you can choose to play and learn to play better. This book can help you become more versatile and make better choices, armed with an expanded repertoire of possibilities. Wizard and warrior images are metaphors to help you think on your feet. When, for example, you are in dangerous and highly charged political situations, what are your options? We will provide examples of three kinds of warrior—toxic, relentless, and principled—and feature exemplars who highlight the costs and benefits of each stance. We will also examine the key attributes that warriors need to be successful—mind, heart, skill, and weapons.

When the culture of your enterprise needs tweaking or transforming, what are your wisest moves? We identify three wizardly roles—authentic, wannabe, and harmful—and demonstrate how leaders can inspire, deflate, or destroy a company. To be successful, wizards need to discover their own magic and spiritual core and then summon the collective spirit through example, values, ritual, ceremony, and stories.

We will study defining moments in the lives of famous and not-so-famous leaders from different eras and places to illuminate pathways to follow and pitfalls to avoid. Those lessons can provide insight and perspective that will be invaluable in your own defining moments. Knowing when to fight or when to invoke key symbols can determine whether you succeed or run aground.

Consider an example of a university leader under fire. Before he became the seventh commissioner of major league baseball, A. Bartlett Giamatti was the president of Yale University. In 1984, he struggled to cope with a divisive strike that was tearing Yale apart. Clerical and technical workers had walked out, demanding higher wages and better benefits. Students and faculty were sharply divided. The strike was taking a heavy toll. A senior Yale administrator described his experience of the strike as "a pressure cooker, just terrible, horrible. Sheer utter hell."[4] Giamatti was feeling the heat:

> No human being enjoys having to have a bodyguard to walk around the campus. No human being enjoys having his family subjected to the kinds of things mine were. No human being enjoys being held up to contempt and ridicule. But no human being who confronts that and then changes all his beliefs about what the place stands for and how money is allocated would be worth very much.[5]

Talk-show host Phil Donahue called President Giamatti with a provocative invitation: Why not bring the whole mess on my show? Lacking obviously better options, Giamatti replied, "Why not?"

Donahue's show often pitted two sides of a heated controversy against one another, with the host acting as provocateur. In the show's first segment, Donahue went after the union and subjected union reps to audience reactions. Next, Giamatti was put on the hot seat. He faced poking and prodding first from Donahue and then from the audience. There were both supporters and opponents, but the opposition was more vocal. Giamatti was barraged with angry criticism. Like a good warrior he took the blows and responded with well-placed jabs. He continually emphasized that university resources were in short supply and that many demands, including those of the strikers, had to be tallied against a finite financial pot. In the give-and-take between Giamatti and the audience it became clear that there were no villains, only distinct interests with legitimate claims. But politically, how could all be satisfied when there wasn't enough to go around? Some unifying thread was needed.

At the end of the show, each side got one minute for a summation. Giamatti was first, and opened by acknowledging the legitimacy of both sides. Then he switched roles from pugilistic warrior to poetic wizard. His language and posture changed as he launched into a story he had never before told in public. His father, Valentine Giamatti, was a son of Italian immigrants who spoke no English when he started grade school, but eventually became a strong student. When Valentine graduated from high school, he had two options: take a job in a local factory or go to school at the local college, which happened to be Yale. He was able to choose the latter only because Yale admitted people based on ability and supported them according to their needs. Passion in his voice, Giamatti underscored the ability-need formula as a core value that would never be sacrificed to short-term demands so long as he was president. The magic worked. The union returned to work later that month. The tape of the program was circulated widely—to alumni and friends of Yale and turned into one of Yale's most effective fundraising appeals.

Giamatti's transition from warrior to wizard is only one illustration of the power of shifting from one role to the other as the situation demands. That becomes easier as you deepen your appreciation of both options. One goal of this book is to enhance your ability to think clearly about the leadership terrain. But thinking is not enough. Cognition and emotion are tightly interwoven. Any perspective on leadership and organizations has both a positive side and a shadow. When they confuse larger purposes with personal desires, adroit politicians can become self-serving tyrants and inspirational leaders can deteriorate into charlatans. To avoid such risks, leaders must look within themselves to recognize urges, fears, and tensions that can sustain, distort, or undermine their well-intended efforts. They must recognize a paradoxical truth: only when they acknowledge and accept the shadow within, the darker impulses that they often deny to themselves and others, can they become whole as leaders.

Leaders who balance their inner warrior and wizard can provide leadership that makes a real and positive difference. When they embrace the political and symbolic aspects of their work, they enable their organizations to flourish and perform. In the chapters to come, we will take a guided tour of the inner workings of these two domains, examining what it means to lead as wizard and warrior. All of us, in different ways and degrees, have within us possibilities for both combat and magic. They become powerful gifts when we learn to recognize and use them.

1

LIGHT AND SHADOW

Mother Teresa and Richard Nixon

Light and dark, good and evil dance together in both our internal and external worlds. Denying their interplay blocks our energy, distorts reality, and leads us into unnecessary traps and tensions. Knowing and acknowledging their coexistence lets us access their power in the service of worthy values and purposes. Two famous leaders—one who died reviled, the other revered— show us what's at stake. Consider first the tortured path of President Richard Nixon.

RICHARD NIXON: WOUNDED WARRIOR

After serving eight years as vice president under Dwight Eisenhower, Richard Nixon narrowly lost his first try for the White House to the younger, more charismatic Jack Kennedy. Then things soured even more. Nixon's attempt at a political comeback crashed when he lost his bid to become governor of California. That prompted an embittered Nixon to make his famous promise that the press wouldn't have him to kick around anymore. He and almost everyone else believed his political career was over.[6] But he nursed his wounds, rebuilt his political ties, and came back from oblivion to win the presidency in 1968 and again in 1972.

Among those who went to work for him was a young and optimistic David Gergen. Fresh from a stint in the U.S. Navy, he arrived at the Nixon White House in January 1970. His job was to assist Nixon's chief speechwriter, Ray Price. In his first months, Gergen rarely saw the brilliant, aloof, and intimidating president he served. But Price had known Nixon for years and willingly shared his insights about the maelstrom of forces swirling within the president's psyche. Gergen recalls, "Nixon, Price explained, was blessed with a very bright side, but mostly hidden from public view was a dark, thunderous aspect. Within the White House, a titanic struggle was under way between those who naturally appealed to his better qualities and those who played upon his demons. Our job, he said, was to strengthen his positive instincts."[7]

Ray Price and others on the presidential staff saw Nixon's potential for greatness but worried about the darker angels in his nature. These often rendered him insecure, secretive, angry, and vindictive. They made Nixon receptive to those on his staff who warned him about his enemies' evil deeds and urged him to take direct, even brutal steps to retaliate. "Nixon would easily succumb and lash out at his foes, real and imagined. If that side ultimately prevailed, Ray warned, the Nixon presidency was doomed."[8]

Ray Price's forebodings ultimately materialized in Nixon's self-destructive spiral following the "third-rate burglary" at the Watergate apartments in Washington. After an ill-advised and bungled foray into political espionage by campaign operatives, Nixon stonewalled investigators. The cover-up failed, leading to personal disgrace and a national tragedy. Fascinating and shadowy, brilliant and petty, loved and hated, Nixon stands out as one of America's most controversial and cryptic presidents. As the only individual ever to resign America's highest office, he is conspicuously one of a kind. Yet the source of his fall—inability to recognize and manage competing demons—is the stuff of Shakespearian tragedy, a story repeated worldwide throughout history. Nixon's demons lurk in even the best of us. Few are aware of how deeply they haunted one of the most beloved and admired figures of the twentieth century, Mother Teresa, the "Angel of Calcutta." As her Vatican biographer puts it:

> Hidden from all eyes, hidden even from those closest to her, was her interior life marked by an experience of a deep, painful and abiding feeling of being separated from God, even rejected by Him, along with an ever-increasing longing for His love. She called her inner experience, "the darkness." The "painful night" of her soul, which began around the time she started her work for the poor and continued to the end of her life, led Mother Teresa to an ever more profound union with God. Through the darkness she mystically participated in the thirst of Jesus, in His painful and burning longing for love, and she shared in the interior desolation of the poor.[9]

MOTHER TERESA: THE ANGEL OF CALCUTTA

Mother Teresa was born Agnes Gonxha Bojaxhiu in 1910 to an Albanian Catholic family in the ancient city of Skopje, Macedonia. As a child she heard a call from God. At age eighteen, she left home to join the Sisters of Loreto, an Irish religious community with missions in India. From 1931 to 1948 she taught at a Catholic high school in Calcutta, eventually becoming its principal. But, during a train ride in 1946, she received her "call within a call"—a direct invitation from Jesus to serve the "poorest of the poor." In 1948, she received permission to leave the convent to pursue her new calling. Alone and without funding, she began her new mission. Daily, she went into the slums, looking for opportunities to provide care and love to those in greatest need.

Gradually, she began to attract followers, including some of her former students. In 1950, she established a new Catholic religious order, the Missionaries of Charity. The order eventually built missions worldwide to carry out its commitment of serving the poor. By her death in 1997, she had become an inspiration to the world for her commitment to doing "small things with great love."

Why would such a saintly woman feel chronic emotional pain? Why would she harbor a prolonged feeling of separation, even rejection from God? She, like Richard Nixon, had her darker side. Admired by most, she also attracted critics who argued that the saintly Mother was a self-promoter who perennially inflated her achievements, harmed people she claimed to help, and stubbornly refused to account for millions of dollars in donations she received over the years.[10] Her estimates of numbers of people served and abortions avoided in Calcutta varied from one occasion to another and appeared to significantly stretch the truth. She ensured that her dying patients, regardless of their religion, were baptized (to give them, in her words, "a ticket to St. Peter"), yet she provided haphazard medical care and emphasized prayer over pain relief.

How does a woman with few worldly resources, working among outcasts, win a Nobel Prize and the adulation of millions worldwide? Mother Teresa gave credit to God, but she helped the work along. She was a politician as well as a saint. Her passion and faith were deep and powerful. They fueled and sustained her commitment to her calling. But her impulses toward power and self-promotion were equally robust. Her political inclinations were at the heart of her spiritual struggles.

The "painful night" of her soul emerged during her decision to leave her spiritual and vocational home, the Sisters of Loreto and the school in Calcutta. Between the two she had devoted almost half her life. It was an agonizing choice, opposed by many of her superiors in the Catholic Church. It required her to back out of her promise of a lifetime commitment to the Sisters of Loreto. How much her decision was fueled by a call from God and how much by her own ambition is unclear. Both played a role. But the godly-worldly tension haunted her and made her who she was.

Richard Nixon and Mother Teresa were larger-than-life world figures, and both struggled to manage the conflicting forces in their psyches. Egged on by short-sighted advisers, Nixon let his ambition and his fears trump his genius, with devastating results. Mother Teresa's triumph was to turn similar tensions into a powerful creative force. She successfully rode the tiger of conflicting impulses and aligned them in support of her call to serve the poor. Their divergent stories reveal deep truths about the risks and possibilities of leadership. Magic and power coexist in the world and in each of us. So too do self-interest and ambition. The forces of light and dark are uniformly real and powerful. Both are at the core of human existence. In the movies we see and novels we read, we rarely encounter anything else. Yet, as much as we are drawn to vicarious experience of others' struggles, we often deny the same troubling tensions in our own lives.

Many of us hope to lead from our comfort zones. We deny our demons and avoid the inevitable tensions between passion and politics. We disavow both warrior and wizard, hoping that expertise and people skills will get us where we want to go. It is a vain hope. In limiting ourselves and playing it safe, we lose touch with reality and close off access to our deeper psychic and spiritual power. We also forfeit the likelihood that we will achieve anything interesting or important. In the short run, as leaders we may feel less pain and anxiety, but the escape is temporary and organizations suffer because what could make a difference is shunted aside. To lead with passion and conviction, we need to embrace both power and spirit. We need to recognize and follow a path of paradox and contradiction, a promising route right in front of us. Yet because of our limited vision it is never easy to find or follow. This book is both a prod and a guide.

2

ASSESSING YOUR INNER WIZARD AND WARRIOR

Years ago, a cigarette brand built a famous advertising campaign around the tag line, "I'd rather fight than switch." The slogan's commercial purpose was fleeting, but it captured a chronic leadership conundrum: when to fight, and when to search for new options. That choice is at the heart of this book. We hope to engage you in reflection about how you currently cope with this dilemma, and how you might approach it differently in the future.

*T*o begin the process, fill out the inventory that follows. It has two purposes: one is to highlight coming attractions—a brief introduction to the basic leadership options this book explores. The second goal is to provide a snapshot of how you lead—at least as you see yourself.

The "Leadership Images" survey contains twelve items. Each asks you to rank order four different possibilities. Give a 4 to the option that is *most like you.* Not the one that you like or agree with most, but the one that you think comes closest to describing you. Give a 3 to the one that is next most like you, and on down to 1 for the option that is least like you. In some cases, you may find it hard to choose because none of the options, or all of the options, seem like you. In such cases, don't agonize. Make your best guess and move on. You can always go back and revise later.

Here's how to compute your scores: Add up all the "a's" (1a + 2a + 3a on through 12a) to get your Analyst score. Add up all the "b's" to get your Caregiver score, all the "c's" for your Warrior score, and all the "d's" for your Wizard score. Each score should be in a range from 12 to 48. Once you have all four, check to see that they total to 120. If not, check your work. Then you can plot your scores on the following chart. If you connect the dots, you will get a more or less kite-shaped figure that provides a visual image of how you rated yourself on the survey.

LEADERSHIP IMAGES:
A LEADERSHIP SELF-INVENTORY

1. I see myself as

4 ___4__ a. Logical

2 ___3__ b. Loving

3 ___1__ c. Combative

1 ___2__ d. Imaginative

2. People would say I am more like

4 ___4__ a. A judge

3 ___3__ b. A counselor

2 ___2__ c. A soldier

1 ___1__ d. A poet

3. The career that suits me best is

1 ___1__ a. Accounting

3 ___3__ b. Teaching

2 ___4__ c. Politics

4 ___2__ d. Design

4. My strongest skills are

4 __4__ a. Analytic

3 __2__ b. Interpersonal

2 __1__ c. Competitive

1 __3__ d. Artistic

5. I enjoy spending free time

1 __2__ a. Managing finances

3 __4__ b. Relaxing with family or friends

2 __1__ c. Competing for victory

4 __3__ d. Creating something

6. The best way to describe me is

3 __4__ a. Technical expert

2 __3__ b. Caring listener

1 __2__ c. Tireless competitor

4 __1__ d. Inspirational leader

7. If I had lived five hundred years ago, I think I would have been

4 __3__ a. A Merchant

2 __4__ b. A Shepherd

3 __2__ c. A Warlord

1 __1__ d. A Magician

8. What has helped me be successful is my ability to

3 __3__ a. Make good decisions

2 __4__ b. Help others be their best

1 __2__ c. Win

4 __1__ d. See possibilities others don't see

9. I am

4 _4_ a. A Realist

3 _3_ b. A Humanist

1 _1_ c. A Battler

2 _2_ d. An Idealist

10. I am best at

4 _3_ a. Clear thinking

2 _4_ b. Caring for others

3 _1_ c. Overcoming opposition

1 _2_ d. Magic

11. People see me as

3 _1_ a. Organized

1 _3_ b. Kind

2 _2_ c. Courageous

4 _4_ d. Wise

12. I am

4 _4_ a. An Analyst

3 _3_ b. A Caregiver

1 _1_ c. A Warrior

2 _2_ d. A Wizard

Totals

_37_ Analyst _39_ Caregiver _20_ Warrior _24_ Wizard

39   29   23   29

120

LEADERSHIP IMAGES CHART

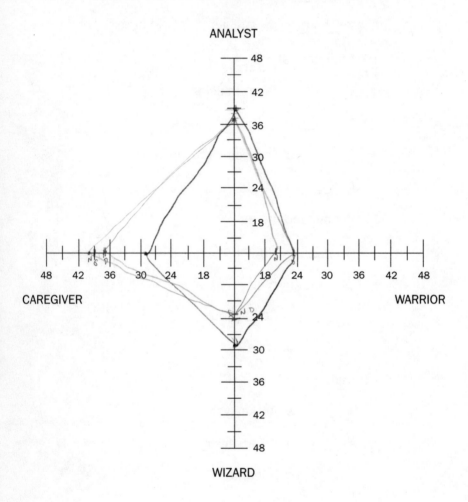

The Leadership Images inventory assesses four different roles for leadership:

1. *Analysts emphasize rationality, analysis, logic, facts, and data.*

They believe that leaders must get the right information, analyze it correctly, and develop goals and strategy based on the facts. They try to avoid or control emotions and politics to avoid distorted decisions and irrational action. They believe a good leader is knowledgeable, thinks clearly, makes the right decisions, has good analytic skills, and can design clear structures and systems that get the job done.

2. *Caregivers emphasize the importance of people and relationships.*

They prefer collaboration to competition and care as much about helping as winning. They look for ways to understand and respond to the needs, concerns, and feelings of colleagues and constituents. They believe in leadership built around coaching, participation, motivation, teamwork, and good interpersonal relations. A good leader cares deeply about others and is a facilitator who listens, supports, and empowers.

3. *Warriors believe that managers and leaders live in a world of conflict and scarce resources.*

The leader's job is mobilizing the resources needed to advocate and fight for the organization's agenda. Warriors emphasize the importance of building a power base: allies, resources, networks, coalitions. They welcome battle and competition rather than fear or avoid it. They are eager to challenge those who oppose their group and its interests. They will protect the group when it is attacked and take the fight to the opposition when the prospects for victory are favorable.

4. *Wizards bring imagination, insight, creativity, vision, meaning, and magic to the work of leadership.*

They look beyond the surface of things to see new possibilities. They surprise and delight followers with new and imaginative solutions to old problems. They goad others to be creative. They often work magic—accomplishing the impossible. They are visionaries with a flair for drama and a yen for symbols who get people excited and committed to the organization's culture and mission. The symbolic tools of their trade include icons, ritual, ceremony, and stories.

These four images correlate with four organizational frames we have written about in earlier books.[11] The Analyst hews to the structural frame, which sees organizations as factories or machines, and focuses on their rational aspects. The Caregiver prefers the human resource frame, with its emphasis on alignment between people and organizations. The Warrior corresponds to the political frame, which sees organizations as arenas in which individuals and groups compete for power and scarce resources. Finally, the Wizard aligns with the symbolic frame, with its emphasis on the cultural and nonrational features of organization.

All four frames are critical for understanding life in groups, organizations, and societies. This book will focus on the warrior and wizard roles because they are the most neglected and the most important for leadership. Our research over the last two decades has consistently found a paradox: most managers rely primarily on the structural and human resource perspectives, *but* the political and symbolic frames are most often associated with effective leadership.[12] Our work suggests that a high percentage of managers are repelled or frightened by the warrior and puzzled by the wizard. As a result they shy away from embracing the possibilities and powers embodied in these images. For those who dislike or fear combat, as is true of many caregivers, recognizing the warrior within is both frightening and disturbing. For analysts who pride themselves on logic and common sense, the wizard's mysterious ways are repellent.

Our hope is to encourage readers to move beyond their initial impulses and explore the images of both warrior and wizard as new possibilities and even new identities. The better you understand both the pitfalls and potentials of these two images, the less you need to fear them. Shunning combat and magic carries a high price—forfeiting much of the power and passion that fuel true leadership. The better people understand and use the possibilities of the wizard and warrior within, the more likely they are to become leaders who bring clout, hope, and faith to organizations that have become neutered and sterile.

Treat the inventory as a starting point for reflection about how you see yourself as a leader. In the chapters to come, we will explore in depth the leadership worlds of both wizard and warrior: what drives them, how they think, and what they do. We will examine when they are effective, when they are not, and how to develop the capabilities and benefits of both.

PART TWO

WARRIOR ROLES

Toxic, Relentless, and Principled

Whether warriors build or destroy depends on how and why they fight. In Part Two, we study three distinct roles that warriors may play, each falling somewhere in the murky terrain between the idealized knights and villainous ogres of legend and fiction. The role an individual plays is determined by a combination of history, character, and circumstance. Recognizing the characteristics and consequences of each warrior role increases your ability to choose one that fits a given situation, and to shift from one to another as circumstances change.

Choosing a role requires finding clarity and direction amid turmoil. Leaders and warriors live in a vortex of opposing forces. Internally, they must struggle to balance conflicting impulses—love of self and love of others, competition and collaboration, creating and destroying, loyalty to oneself or to a greater cause. Externally, they must contend with conflicting expectations embodied in two pervasive images of the warrior. One is the hero, the champion who fights noble battles. The hero is a principled warrior who fights from necessity rather than desire, always seeking justice, truth, and peace. The darker image is embodied in the villain—an evil alien who fights for power and dominion, cruelly seeking to destroy good people and their way of life. The tension between these two archetypes is pervasive throughout history, legend, fiction, and film. The list of encounters is endless—David and Goliath, Hamlet and his usurping stepfather, Joan of Arc and her enemies, Luke Skywalker and Darth Vader, Harry Potter and Lord Voldemort.

Sometimes our unscrupulous enemy is someone else's perfect knight. In the wake of 9/11, Osama bin Laden became one of the most hated figures in the Western world. Yet he was a hero to many in North Africa, the Middle East, and Asia, who displayed his picture in places of honor. All leaders make enemies as well as friends. They inevitably generate mixed reactions and ambivalence, so it is a mistake to take too much comfort from the praise of allies or suffer too much pain from the attacks of enemies. Ares, the Greek god of war, was the son of Zeus and Hera, both of whom hated him. In the *Iliad*, Homer describes Ares as "murderous, blood-stained, the incarnate curse of mortals," and "strangely, a coward, too."[13] Like warriors before and since, Ares was loved and hated, worshiped by some and reviled by others.

The warrior's choice of role is further complicated by a persistent tension between noble aspirations and tedious realities. Warriors are frequently wedged between the sublime and the mundane, between lofty imperatives of a demanding ethical code and constant temptations of baser, more expedient interests. This struggle arises in part from the gap between patriotic dreams and the grim reality of the battlefield. It also reflects the transitory nature of human life—we are all dust on the wind. Death may come suddenly. Since there is little time to waste, warriors are perennially tempted to grab what they can while they can.

Finally, the role warriors play depends on the cause they seek. For some the cause is narrow and selfish. Others commit themselves to a larger common good. There have been many warrior leaders in war, politics, and business. Most have claimed to fight on behalf of some noble mission. Far fewer have ultimately succeeded in achieving great purposes and accomplishing their chosen agenda. Too many accumulate power and then use it badly, unleashing destructive forces that lead to waste and ruin. The table at the end of this section presents some examples of people filling the various warrior roles.

At the destructive end of the warrior continuum, we find the *toxic warrior*, whose inner world is dominated by conflict and turmoil. In toxic warriors, the conflict between forces of dark and light rages with almost unmanageable intensity. They are, at worst, thugs and sadists. They believe that victory and their own interests supersede everything else. They have little patience for ethical concerns; the end justifies the means. They are often brilliant, politically shrewd, and charismatic. They may temporarily achieve extraordinary heights, yet their truncated vision and moral flaws lead almost inevitably to tragedy. Adolph Hitler, Joseph Stalin, and Pol Pot exemplify the most destructive of toxic warriors. Each amassed extraordinary power and changed history, but left a legacy of damage and death. Their commercial cousins include people like Leona Helmsley and "Chainsaw" Al Dunlap.

Midway on the continuum is the *relentless warrior*—a tireless and passionate battler. Like their toxic counterparts, these warriors want to win, but they recognize that some costs are too high. They will push the rules of the game only so far. Microsoft founder Bill Gates, U.S. President George W. Bush, and Hewlett-Packard's embattled CEO Carly Fiorina are among many examples of the relentless warrior.

Nearer the light end of the continuum, we find *principled warriors.* They see victory as a means rather than an end, worthy only if honorable and in service of a higher purpose. Mary Kay Ash, Abraham Lincoln, and legendary basketball coach John Wooden are examples.

In the coming chapters, we will examine each of these roles, highlighting lessons from successes and failures of leaders who have done great things as well as others who have produced great tragedy.

EXAMPLES OF WARRIOR ROLES

LEADERSHIP POSITION	TOXIC	RELENTLESS	PRINCIPLED
Business chief executives	Al Dunlap	Bill Gates	Warren Buffett
Military leaders	Hermann Goëring	Ulysses S. Grant	George Marshall
American presidents	Richard Nixon	George W. Bush	Abraham Lincoln
Basketball coaches	Bobby Knight	Mike Krzyzewski	John Wooden

3

THE TOXIC WARRIOR

History is filled with tales of implacable warriors who conquered territories, destroyed cities, and massacred thousands. Attila the Hun and Genghis Khan come readily to mind. Toxic warriors are often tragic figures who destroy more than they create. The fires of ambition burn too hot. These leaders are intoxicated by their own visions of grandeur and come to believe that they can do whatever they want. They exemplify Chris Hedges's view of war as a force that provides meaning by replacing life's confusion and aimlessness with an exclusive and exhilarating goal of victory and destroying one's enemies.[14] The recent spate of toxic leaders in the business community has triggered many studies of pathological leadership.[15] Manfred Kets de Vries talks about narcissistic leaders who are driven by a selfish need for admiration and adulation but give little back in return.[16] Barbara Kellerman's typology of bad leaders includes three types that qualify as toxic warriors: the *callous* (who have no concern about others' needs), the *corrupt* (who will lie, cheat, and steal), and the *evil* (who inflict severe psychic or physical damage on others).[17]

LEONA HELMSLEY: "THE QUEEN OF MEAN"

The business world has produced many toxic warriors, some famous, others more obscure. One of the most notorious was Leona Helmsley. Her marriage to real estate tycoon Harry Helmsley was her passport to command the lavish new Helmsley Palace Hotel in New York City. She had been a highly successful real estate agent, selling high-end properties to New York's upper crust. She had no history in the hotel business or as a manager. Her primary qualification was that Harry loved her. She positioned herself in an ad campaign as the queen who stood guard at the palace gate. It worked with customers, but her management style was devastating to staff. She demanded perfection, but operated as if she believed that the more she abused her employees, the better they would perform. When abuse didn't work, she tried fits of rage. She screamed insults and profanities at workers and managers and fired people on the spot for specks of lint or dirty fingernails. She was so widely feared and hated that her minions called her the Queen of Mean.[18] Eventually, the fear and loathing in the ranks stimulated an inside tip to prosecutors about shady financial dealings. Many felt Helmsley got what she deserved when she was sentenced to twenty-one months for tax evasion.[19] (Her husband was saved by senility—he was judged too weak physically and mentally to stand trial.)

"CHAINSAW" AL DUNLAP

While it isn't easy to surpass Helmsley's levels of toxicity, "Chainsaw" Al Dunlap managed to do even more damage on a broader scale. Brilliant, arrogant, and pugnacious, Dunlap rose in the 1990s to become America's king of turnaround artists. His fame turned his leadership secrets into a business best-seller with the provocative title *Mean Business: How I Save Bad Companies and Make Good Companies Great.* Dunlap had been combative in childhood. He was so difficult that he and his family disowned one another. His first wife, filing for divorce, alleged that his abusive behavior included throwing her to the floor and threatening her with a kitchen knife. After an undistinguished career at West Point and three years in the military, Dunlap went into business and worked his way up the management ladder. He quickly developed a reputation for hard work, decisiveness, and plenty of pink slips. It seemed that wherever he went, jobs shriveled but profits bloomed.

He cemented his reputation as a corporate messiah during his tenure as chief executive of Scott Paper, where he more than doubled profits and market value. He achieved this financial miracle by slashing head count and cutting "frills" like research and development. For good measure, he told managers not to get involved in community activities, eliminated all corporate contributions to charity, and moved Scott's headquarters from Philadelphia (where it had been for more than a century) to Boca Raton, Florida (where Dunlap had a new home).

Analysts and shareholders loved the impact on the bottom line. A closer look revealed that employee morale sank and Scott lost market share in every major product line. Dunlap did not stay long enough to find out whether he had sacrificed Scott's future for short-term gains. After less than two years, he sold the company to its biggest competitor and walked away with almost $100 million. On the same day that officials in Boca Raton, Florida, received Dunlap's request for a $156,000 incentive grant for job creation, Scott's new owners announced that the Boca Raton headquarters would close.[20]

Despite his questionable legacy at Scott, Dunlap attracted a large following, including Sunbeam Corporation's board of directors. Sunbeam had a strong brand name but had been adrift for years. Sunbeam hired Dunlap in mid-1996 to work his managerial skills on its struggling appliance business. The market saw it as a brilliant move: the stock price jumped 50 percent the day Dunlap was hired. Promising 20 percent annual gains in revenues and profits, Dunlap started with a vengeance. He laid off about half of Sunbeam's workforce and closed more than half of the company's factories and warehouses. Even some analysts had doubts about such a draconian shrink-your-way-to-success approach. Inside Sunbeam, anyone who voiced concerns was soon out of a job.

For more than a year, Dunlap's strategy appeared to work. In a way, it worked too well. Sunbeam's stock soared so high Dunlap couldn't follow his usual script—sell fast and get out while he was ahead. The company had gone from the doldrums to overpriced, and no one was willing to pay what the market said Sunbeam was worth. That forced Dunlap to stick around and manage the company. He bravely declared victory in late 1997, but things were already falling apart. To prop up the company's 1997 numbers, Sunbeam pushed off-season merchandise out the door, offering discounted, buy-now-pay-later prices on electric blankets in the summer and barbecue grills in December. Mortgaging future sales only delayed the inevitable: a big splash of red ink, and a free fall in the stock price in early 1998. Things continued downhill from there. Dunlap, despite his self-image as "Rambo in pinstripes," tried to pin the blame on El Niño and assorted enemies. His board didn't buy it. With the company teetering toward bankruptcy, they sacked him less than two years after he came aboard.

WARDING OFF TOXICITY

Dunlap and Helmsley, like many toxic leaders, were classic narcissists:

> Notwithstanding his occasional illusions of omnipotence, the narcis-
> sist depends on others to validate his self-esteem. He cannot live
> without an admiring audience. His apparent freedom from family ties
> and institutional constraints does not free him to stand alone or to
> glory in his individuality. On the contrary, it contributes to his inse-
> curity, which he can overcome only by seeing his "grandiose self"
> reflected in the attentions of others.[21]

But circumstances also nudged Helmsley and Dunlap into the toxic warrior role. Helmsley's perfectionism and fanatically high standards might have been a virtue in a luxury hotel had she possessed the leadership skills and experience to develop employee buy-in. Lacking more productive strategies, she relied on temper tantrums and yelling to motivate people, which created a destructive climate of fear and loathing. Likewise, under different circumstances, Dunlap's pugnacity might not have become as toxic, but he came of age in an era when the business and investment communities were relentlessly focused on the bottom line and short-term results. If the quarterly earnings go up, you're a hero. Otherwise, you're a bum. Like the chief financial officers at Enron and WorldCom, Dunlap went to extremes with strategies designed to do the in thing: report good earnings and boost the stock price.

AVOIDING THE TOXIC ROLE

The path of the toxic warrior is tragic for everyone. Avoiding it is a challenge for both individuals and organizations. A few guidelines can help:

1. *Managers need a realistic sense of self.*

Companies often report that lack of self-awareness is one of the most common causes of career flameouts in the management ranks. That is one reason that 360-degree feedback is so widely used in management development. Feedback, as Blanchard and Johnson wrote years ago, "is the breakfast of champions."[22] Good leaders actively seek feedback about weaknesses as well as strengths because they see it as a learning tool rather than an assault on their self-concept. In practice, this is difficult for toxic leaders, who are often unaware of the psychic inferno that burns within. They project their inner pain and conflict on others—believing that they are surrounded by the weak and the incompetent, and that they alone can bring success to their organization.

2. *Be alert to signs of toxic leadership.*

Most managers see the world as competitive, with good reason. Toxic warriors take that perception to extremes. They feel surrounded by enemies whom they must dominate and defeat. Seeing the world as dangerous, they find it hard to feel comfortable unless they are in full control; the fact that people and events around them often turn out to be uncontrollable only spurs toxic warriors to seek even more power. Finding it almost impossible to admit error, they become angry or enraged when criticized. They carry grudges and nurture impulses for revenge. Individuals who show such traits are at risk. They need assistance, though they may be the last to recognize it. A coach or counselor they can trust may be able to help them listen to their inner dialogue, recognize their blind spots, and begin to develop an appreciation of other leadership possibilities.

3. *Take on a new role.*

It is hard to stop doing something until you have something else to replace it. Toxic warriors are unlikely to give up combat, but they may well be able to move to a more productive stance, such as the relentless warrior role discussed in the next chapter. Trying on new roles expands the palette of possibilities. Leaders gravitate to the toxic warrior mode when a confluence of circumstances and their own propensities pushes them toward a scorched-earth model of leadership. If it works, which it might in the short term, they become consumed with an insatiable desire for power coupled with an unshakeable confidence in the rightness of their own agenda. Toxic warriors can be charming and highly skilled at arm twisting and manipulation, but deep down, they care little about anyone's interests other than their own. As with Leona Helmsley and Al Dunlap, their career arc often begins with a meteoric rise, followed by an equally rapid free fall. They mostly leave a legacy of tragedy and destruction. It is a path well worth avoiding.

4

THE RELENTLESS WARRIOR

Toxic warriors fight because they don't see other options—life is war, and demons within propel them into battle. *Relentless* warriors also have demons, but their hunger for combat is more disciplined. Relentless warriors are passionate about their aims. But they are pragmatic enough to know the dangers of plunging recklessly over legal or ethical cliffs. Unlike the principled warriors discussed in Chapter Five, they are gamesmen rather than moral philosophers. They often test and sometimes bend the rules but rarely break them. High-profile cases have shown that you lose if your actions put you in jail, or if the products of your enterprise cause death or injury. One relentless warrior, a successful entrepreneur, summarized his perspective on business ethics very simply: "Death and jail scare me."

The boundary between toxic and relentless warriors is nebulous, and leaders may alternate between one role and the other. General George S. Patton, one of the most brilliant military leaders in World War II, was primarily a relentless warrior. But in the face of disappointment or frustration, he sometimes veered toward a more toxic mode. Charismatic and swashbuckling, Patton continually struggled to control his emotional volatility. During the Allied campaign in Sicily, he lost that tussle on a famous occasion. He met a young soldier hospitalized for what might now be labeled post-traumatic stress syndrome. Patton asked him what was wrong. The soldier, beginning to cry, replied, "It's my nerves, sir." The idea of leaving the front for a mere psychic wound was repugnant for the general. "Your nerves hell!" Patton shouted back. "You are just a Goddamn coward!"[23] The general slapped the young man in the face, told him to shut up his "damn crying," and then slapped him again.

Patton could have been court-martialed. His superior, Dwight Eisenhower, came under heavy pressure to relieve him. Eisenhower agonized over what do to, and then wrote to Patton, saying he could not excuse "brutality, abuse of the sick or uncontrollable temper in front of subordinates."[24] But Ike was looking ahead to D-Day, and he felt no other combat commander could equal Patton's record under fire. Patton apologized dutifully to the soldier, but kept his command.

The qualities of the relentless warrior consistently appear among the entrepreneurs who build great business enterprises. Kodak founder George Eastman was a warrior as well as an innovator. "Peace extends only to private life," he observed, "In business it is war all the time."[25] John D. Rockefeller's relentless drive to dominate oil refining eventually put him in control of more than 90 percent of the industry. He used this commanding position to tighten the squeeze on his few remaining competitors. He pressured railroads into a secret agreement that gave him a rebate of twenty cents on every barrel of oil that he or his competitors shipped.[26] As a young man, Cornelius Vanderbilt on occasion defended his business interests with his fists. In his later years, he was less physical but no less combative. On one famous occasion, some associates tried to wrest control of his company while he was away on business. He fired off a famous letter:

> *Gentlemen:*
> *You have undertaken to cheat me. I won't*
> *sue you, for the law is too slow. I'll ruin you.*
> *Yours truly,*
> *Cornelius Vanderbilt*[27]

Ruin them he did.

John D. Rockefeller's oil monopoly was eventually broken up by government trust-busters. Successors of this federal posse tried to do the same thing more than a century later to the Rockefeller of the personal computer industry—Bill Gates. Rockefeller was smart and tough, but he was also charming and had a reputation for integrity. He took over his industry by buying out his competitors, and, as one of them put it, "He treated everybody fairly. When we sold out, he gave us a fair price." Gates is at least as smart, but fair is not the word that comes to his competitors' minds to describe him:

> "Competing with Bill Gates," moaned Mitch Kapor of Lotus, "is like putting your head in a vise and turning the handle. He doesn't take no for an answer and he keeps coming back." Philippe Kahn of Borland International was even more explicit. "When you deal with Gates," he complained, "you feel raped."[28]

BILL GATES: THE RELENTLESS GEEK

Bill Gates was in the right place in the early 1980s when IBM's fledgling personal computer business was searching for an operating system. Gates didn't have one, but his partner, Paul Allen, knew someone who did. Gates paid $75,000 for QDOS (Quick and Dirty Operating System) in the deal—or steal—of the twentieth century. Gates changed the name to DOS and resold it to IBM, shrewdly retaining the right to license it to anyone else. DOS quickly became the primary operating system for most of the world's personal computers. And Gates was on his way to becoming one of the world's richest men.[29]

Even as a twenty-year-old, when he dropped out of Harvard to become CEO of a tiny software firm then known as Micro-Soft, Gates displayed many of the traits of the warrior entrepreneur. He was a prodigiously hard worker and expected as much from those around him. He set lofty standards and was intolerant of any shortfall. "That's the stupidest thing I've ever heard" was routine feedback in the Gates lexicon. He attacked users over the issue of software piracy, writing blunt letters to hobbyist publications that spawned many enemies in the fledgling geek community. Gates also took a scorched-earth approach to competitors. He was famous for heading off rivals' new products by announcing unrealistic plans to ship a Microsoft offering better and sooner. Shortly before Apple debuted its splashy graphic interface for the Macintosh, Gates announced that Microsoft's own graphic offering, Windows, was coming soon. Windows actually appeared a year and a half later than promised, earning Microsoft a "Golden Vaporware Award" from a major computer publication. Unembarrassed, Gates reused the vaporware strategy many times.

Gates's warrior mentality was never clearer than in Microsoft's long battle against one of the biggest antitrust cases of the late twentieth century. In December 1997, while Gates was on a trip to China, word arrived that a federal judge had sided with the government and ordered Microsoft to stop bundling its Internet Explorer browser with Windows. With Gates out of town, the mood at Microsoft's Seattle headquarters was confused and chaotic. But senior executives concluded that it was better to skirt a direct confrontation with the government, and soft-pedal in the hope of turning away the feds' wrath. Gates trashed that diplomatic stance as soon as he returned to the office. In his view, the court's order threatened a nonnegotiable principle, Microsoft's right to design software as it saw fit. Gates took a provocative and uncompromising stance. Microsoft announced that it would offer two versions of Windows: one with Internet Explorer and another without. But sales of the "without" version were expected to be poor, since it was crippled by the removal of files shared between browser and operating system. The ploy infuriated just about everyone. Government lawyers were apoplectic, and an exasperated judge asked a Microsoft lawyer, "It seemed absolutely clear to you that I entered an order that required you to distribute a product that would not work? Is that what you're telling me?"

"In plain English, yes," said the attorney.[30]

Microsoft won the legal battle, but the company took a significant hit in the minds of consumers, many of whom were appalled by its arrogant, damn-the-torpedoes stance. Seven years later, industry observer Mark Anderson commented, "Microsoft's reputation of being nasty and overly aggressive and not a good global citizen severely hurt the brand. It could've been a cakewalk for them as the world moved to smart phones and interactive entertainment, but instead, repairing the damage will take years."[31] Like General Patton, Gates sometimes got carried away by his own combativeness.

CARLY FIORINA: A RELENTLESS WARRIOR UNDER FIRE

One of the business world's most visible women warriors of recent years is Carly Fiorina, chief executive officer of electronics giant Hewlett-Packard until she was forced out early in 2005. (As discussed in a later chapter, Fiorina played the role of would-be wizard as well. Her triumphs and defeats borrowed from both roles.) For much of her life, Fiorina was viewed as a superstar. She was smart, confident, outspoken, and impressively articulate. She was also tough, known for "her willingness to battle ferociously to achieve her goals, whether in closing a sale, winning a job, or pushing through a merger."[32] Like other relentless warriors, she was chronically controversial, leaving in her wake both strong admirers and bitter critics.

Fresh from an MBA program, Fiorina took her first management job at AT&T's Network Systems Division. She rose quickly, developing a reputation as a superlative salesperson: "No one worked harder to understand the customer, the market or the politics inherent in every big deal. She understood how all the company's products and services could be pulled together. She was the one person with the charisma, the contacts, and the determination to corral all of Network Systems' capabilities to meet a customer's needs."[33]

When AT&T decided to spin off Network Systems as a new company called Lucent, Fiorina was promoted to executive vice president and given responsibility for marketing the new company to investors. She had little background in finance, but tackled the assignment with her usual determination, attention to detail, and focus on the customers—in this case, investment bankers. She was a hit. For the next several years, Lucent was a high-flyer in the business world, and Fiorina played a key role in its success. Her reputation attracted the attention of Hewlett-Packard, whose search for a new CEO had been producing lackluster results. Fiorina's star power and ability to light up a room wowed most of HP's board. In July 1999, she got the job.

Once hired, she found herself at the head of a troubled giant. HP was large and profitable, with more than $40 billion in annual revenue. But customer service had been deteriorating while bureaucracy was trumping innovation. A few weeks after she became CEO, *Business Week* described the company as part of "the clueless establishment."[34] Fiorina's arrival was big news for more than one reason. She was only the fifth CEO in HP's sixty-year history, and she was the first to come from outside since Bill (Hewlett) and Dave (Packard) founded the company in a Palo Alto garage in 1938. She was also the first woman to head a company of HP's size in any industry. She brought much strength, including "a silver tongue and an iron will."[35] But she faced daunting challenges, especially after she set her sights on a merger with Compaq Computer, another floundering $40-billion company. Bill and Dave's heirs, who controlled more than 15 percent of HP's stock, didn't like the idea. The battle lines were drawn. Fiorina had to win a massive gunfight at the HP corral or lose her job.

Fiorina knew she needed support from HP's board, from analysts, and ultimately from a majority of voting shares. She first went after board support, but ran into a stroke of bad luck. Bill Hewlett's grandson, Walter, missed the board meeting at which McKinsey consultants made the case for the merger. A month later Hewlett voted reluctantly and under pressure from fellow board members to approve the move. But he had serious misgivings. In his mind, the substantial layoffs that were touted as one of the merger's "synergies" amounted to abandoning the employee-friendly "HP way." His doubts grew when HP's stock dropped some 40 percent after the merger announcement. A few weeks later, he announced that he would vote his shares against the merger.[36] Fiorina now faced an uphill battle. Her job and her vision for HP both rode on the outcome. To win, she had to make a case persuasive enough to win over the thin slice of analysts and shareholders still on the fence.

The primary targets were institutional shareholders, who held more than half the stock, and analysts whose opinions mattered. One analyst with the potential to make or break the deal was Ram Kumar of Institutional Shareholders Services, an advisory firm whose clients held more than a fifth of HP's stock. He was initially skeptical about the deal, but Fiorina's persuasiveness and command of detail won him over. "She was very impressive, Kumar said. "She had a forceful personality, was in total command of the subject matter and always had a strong response."[37]

As the battle intensified, Fiorina even resorted to the business equivalent of political attack ads. HP put out a press release designed to subtly discredit Walter Hewlett as a clueless dilettante: "Walter Hewlett, an heir of HP co-founder Bill Hewlett, is a musician and academic who oversees the Hewlett family trust and foundation. While he serves on HP's board of directors, Walter has never worked at the company or been involved in its management."[38]

The vote came down to the wire, and Fiorina prepared three different press releases, one for a win, one for a loss, and one for a photo finish. She breathed a huge sigh of relief when the merger squeaked through. In the first three years after the Compaq deal closed, Fiorina had a mixture of successes and miscues. Revenues grew, but profits were elusive, and the stock languished. Under growing fire from an array of critics, Fiorina stood her ground, but her board finally forced her out in February 2005.

GEORGE W. BUSH: A RELENTLESS WARRIOR IN THE WHITE HOUSE

Many political leaders with little or no military experience gravitate to the warrior role. One famous example is former British Prime Minister Margaret Thatcher—"the Iron Lady." Thatcher was combative to her core, and she had a larger impact on her country than any prime minister since Winston Churchill. She was a great fan of her contemporary, President Ronald Reagan, because they were ideologically close. But as a leader, she resembled the forty-third U.S. president, George W. Bush. Like Bush, she had a deeply conservative political philosophy, a strong commitment to traditional Christian faith, an unshakeable assurance that her views were right, and an unwavering tenacity in holding her ground against opposition.

Typical of relentless warriors, Thatcher and Bush generated boundless admiration from supporters and intense antipathy from enemies. Bush's opponents saw him as intellectually shallow, dangerously stubborn, and incompetent. To supporters, he was just the sort of plain-talking straight-shooter that America needed in the wake of the 9/11 terrorist attack: "a brave, daring leader riding fearlessly into the unknown, striking out against unseen enemies, pulling his team behind him."[39]

Bush, like others of his ilk, was tenacious and determined, and kept self-doubts, if he had any, under wraps. Relentless warriors believe in their purposes and agenda, and pursue them tirelessly. In the words of David Gergen:

> Bush is a top-down, no-nonsense, decisive, macho leader who sets his eye on the far horizon and doesn't "go wobbly" getting there. He is crisp and can be confrontational, expecting others to follow or get out the way. . . . Once he sets a course, he may try his hand at public persuasion. But if people don't swing behind him, he plunges ahead anyway, trusting that they will catch up later. He has learned through experience that if he and his team repeat a clear, simple message long enough, the public is much more likely to give him permission to act, even if not fully persuaded.[40]

STRENGTHS AND LIMITS OF THE RELENTLESS WARRIOR

1. *Relentless warriors' courage, persistence, and determination make them formidable foes.*

What Eisenhower once concluded about Patton could be said about most relentless warriors: "Patton's strength is that he thinks only in terms of attack as long as there is a single battalion that he can keep advancing."[41] That tenacity enabled Bush, Thatcher, Rockefeller, and Gates to build great businesses or profoundly sway their world.

2. *Relentless warriors excel when the objective is clear and they can advance against clearly defined adversaries.*

Relentless warriors may lose focus in murky situations in which it is hard to define the opposition. After the tragedy of 9/11, Bush was brilliant when he could direct his energies against a specific foe—terrorists who threatened American security. After the devastation of Hurricane Katrina in 2005, when the hostile forces were ill-defined and the most prominent targets were his own appointees, the president appeared hesitant and awkward.

Carly Fiorina was at her best during the scuffle over the Compaq merger, marshaling her allies and resources to squeak out an uphill victory. But she struggled over the misty puzzles of transforming HP from a lumbering giant to a more focused and disciplined business.

Brilliant in war, Patton floundered in peace. After Germany surrendered, Patton lobbied for a combat command in the Pacific, only to be made governor of Bavaria instead. His behavior was so erratic that Eisenhower relieved him within a few months, and ordered him home. Patton never made it. The general who expected to perish in combat died instead from injuries sustained in an automobile accident.

3. *Relentless warriors' constricted field of view, stubbornness, and willingness to steamroller opponents casts them as polarizing figures.*

Unyielding warriors often meet defeat because they spread their forces too thin or continue to fight even when the jig is up. Fiorina, Patton, and Thatcher were finally forced out of office by former allies who could no longer tolerate their excesses and stubbornness.

Relentless warriors wage battle with an unshakeable faith in their own worldviews. They live by the mottos of *never retreat* and *compromise only when your back is against an insurmountable wall*. They make almost as many enemies as friends, but their focus, passion, and persistence often make them leaders of extraordinary impact.

5

THE
PRINCIPLED
WARRIOR

On November 21, 2004, a group of senior officers in the SBU, Ukraine's principal intelligence agency, met in the office of their chief, Colonel General Ihor P. Smeshko. Their government had just announced a fraudulent victory for the president's handpicked successor, Prime Minister Viktor F. Yanukovich. There were massive protests in the streets of Kiev, and the possibility of civil war loomed. Intelligence agencies, particularly those descended from the old Soviet KGB, tend to be instinctively conservative and protective of existing power structures. But the men in the room had little respect for Yanukovich, and they dreaded the prospect of blood spilled in the streets. The key question was what, if anything, they could or should do. General Smeshko put the issue head-on: "Today we can save our faces or our epaulettes, or we can try to save our country."[42]

They chose to save their country. They established underground channels to communicate directly with the opposition. Within the government, they fiercely opposed the use of force against the demonstrators who filled the streets of the nation's capital. The most harrowing moment came on November 27. They learned that an Interior Ministry general had ordered ten thousand riot troops into the city. An SBU colonel went to the main square, prepared to position himself between demonstrators and troops. Meanwhile, Smeshko and his allies frantically worked the phones. They ultimately managed to head off the troops.

Once it became clear that the government would not turn against its people, political and legal initiatives could move forward. Concerted negotiations eventually led to a new election and a new president. To the surprise of many, the spies had played a critical behind-the-scenes role in enabling a peaceful resolution. Faced with the most daunting personal and national crisis he had ever witnessed, General Smeshko chose principle over self-interest. The principle that he and his colleagues put above all others was very simple: "At all times we talked of our desire to prevent the shedding of blood."[43]

Relentless warriors fight because they are passionate about a purpose and love to fight. As George Patton put it, "All real Americans love the sting and clash of battle."[44] Winning becomes an end in itself, a source of genuine satisfaction. Principled warriors are equally passionate about the values they pursue, but see combat as a low-priority means, not a highly attractive end. They fight because they sometimes have to when duty requires it. Patton's boss in World War II, General Dwight Eisenhower, expressed this view unmistakably, saying he seriously doubted that any pacifist detested war more than he did. In Eisenhower's words, he fought because he hated the Nazis even more than he detested war and because "The only unforgivable sin in war is not doing your duty."[45]

ABRAHAM LINCOLN: POOR HATER, PRINCIPLED WARRIOR

Abraham Lincoln, one of history's greatest principled warriors, had no fear of combat, but was once described as "a very poor hater."[46] His difficulty in disliking even his enemies was expressed in the eloquent words of his second inaugural, "with malice toward none, with charity for all." Like Eisenhower, Lincoln hated war, which he referred to as "terrible" and "a mighty scourge."[47] In his first inaugural address (March 4, 1861), Lincoln made it clear he did not want war, but would readily fight to defend a principle. He argued forcefully against war on the practical ground that it was unnecessary and fruit-less: "Suppose you go to war, you cannot fight always; and when, after much loss on both sides, and no gain on either, you cease fighting, the identical old questions as to terms of intercourse are again upon you."[48] He closed with a passionate, poetic plea:

> In your hands, my dissatisfied fellow-countrymen, and not in mine, is the momentous issue of civil war. The Government will not assail you. You can have no conflict without being yourselves the aggressors. You have no oath registered in heaven to destroy the Government, while I shall have the most solemn one to reserve, protect, and defend it. . . . We must not be enemies. Though passion may have strained, it must not break our bonds of affection. The mystic chords of memory, stretching from every battlefield and patriot grave to every living heart and hearthstone all over this broad land, will yet swell the chorus of the Union, when again touched, as surely they will be, by the better angels of our nature.[49]

Growing up in the early nineteenth century in rural Kentucky
and Indiana, Abraham Lincoln seemed always out of sync:

> In a society of hunters, Lincoln did not hunt; where many males shot
> rifles, Lincoln did not shoot; among many who were cruel to animals,
> Lincoln was kind; surrounded by farmers, Lincoln fled from farming;
> in a frontier village preoccupied with physical tasks, Lincoln avoided
> manual labor; in a world in which men smoked and chewed, Lincoln
> never used tobacco; in a rough, profane world, Lincoln did not swear;
> in a hard-drinking society, Lincoln did not drink; in a white world with
> strong racial antipathies, Lincoln was generous to blacks; in an envi-
> ronment indifferent to education, Lincoln cared about it intensely.[50]

Lincoln even looked different—his contemporaries regularly
described him as gawky, homely, bony, lanky, stooped—even down-
right ugly. His arms always seemed too long and his pants too short.
Lincoln also had substantive flaws often glossed over in the glow of
his revered place in America's pantheon of heroes. He was haunted
by self-doubt and periodic bouts of depression.[51] He realized early in
life that he was smarter than most people around him. At times he
was intellectually arrogant. This particularly infuriated those whose
formal education was much beyond his.

He was intensely ambitious and embarked on a political career
to make his mark on the world. His desire for success made him
envious of those who had achieved more than he. His jealously was
particularly evident toward his best-known and longest-running
antagonist, Steven A. Douglas. Lincoln and Douglas first met when
both were young members of the Illinois legislature. But the younger
Douglas had quickly surpassed Lincoln, becoming "what Lincoln
would have liked to be but wasn't: an eminent man, famous throughout the land."[52] The combination of intellectual arrogance, ambition,
and envy surfaced in Lincoln's many sarcastic attacks on Douglas,

including a verbal onslaught during their contest for the U.S. Senate in 1858:

> Senator Douglas is of world-wide renown. All the anxious politicians of his party, or who have been of his party for years past, have been looking upon him as certainly, at no distant day, to be the President of the United States. They have seen in his round, jolly fruitful face, post-offices, land-offices, marshalships and cabinet appointments, chargeships and foreign missions, bursting and sprouting out in wonderful exuberance, ready to be laid hold of by their greedy hands. And as they have been gazing upon this attractive picture so long, they cannot, in the little distraction that has taken place in the party, bring themselves to give up the charming hope; but with greedier anxiety they rush about him, sustain him, and give him marches, triumphal entries, and receptions beyond what even in the days of his highest prosperity they could have brought about in his favor.[53]

Lincoln lost the election, in no small measure because Douglas repeatedly played the 1858 version of the race card. The policy issue in the debates was whether slavery could be extended into new U.S. territories: Lincoln opposed it and Douglas didn't. From the beginning of the campaign Douglas pressed the matter:

> Now, I do not question Mr. Lincoln's sincerity on this point. He believes that the negro, by the divine law, is created the equal of the white man, and that no human law can deprive him of that equality, thus secured; and he contends that the negro ought therefore to have all the rights and privileges of citizenship on an equality with the white man. In order to accomplish this, the first thing that would have to be done in this State would be to blot out of our State Constitution that clause which prohibits negroes from coming into this

State, and making it an African colony, and permit them to come and spread over these charming prairies until in midday they shall look black as night.[54]

Like many politicians before and since, Douglas was well aware that he was playing to the fears and prejudices of his audience. It worked. Lincoln struggled to respond, sometimes inconsistently. In his most troubling efforts to deflect the Douglas attack, he conceded the merits of white superiority: "I, as much as any other man, am in favor of having the superior position assigned to the white race."[55] For remarks like that, Lincoln has been justly criticized as racist or worse. He wanted to win, and some of his remarks were more marked by political expediency than centered on a clear moral position. But even though we might wish that the Lincoln of 1858 had been more saintly, it is equally important that Lincoln consistently framed slavery as an ethical issue. The main point of disagreement with Douglas was that Lincoln insisted slavery was wrong, while Douglas refused to take a position. Lincoln continually returned to his bedrock belief in a principle clearly enunciated in the Declaration of Independence—all men are created equal. Douglas claimed that the phrase applied only to white men.

Like all leaders, Lincoln was a creature of his time. But he grew intellectually and morally as he matured, and became a highly principled warrior. He worked tirelessly to embed issues in a larger philosophical and moral framework. He battled courageously for the principles he considered essential to an American way of life.

Much of the nation was startled when Lincoln won the Republican nomination and the presidency in the election of 1860. At the time, he held no office and had lost more elections than he'd won, including the loss to Douglas two years earlier. "An unknown railroad lawyer from an upstart party,"[56] he was known mostly through his speeches. But they were extraordinary—in their precision of argument, intellectual depth, and above all their moral clarity. He gave more cogent and impassioned voice than anyone else to the core conviction that had given birth to the Republican party only a few years before—that slavery was fundamentally wrong.

Lincoln's beliefs would be tested further. Within six weeks of his election, South Carolina voted to secede from the Union, followed in short order by six other states. Lincoln was privately supportive of efforts to keep the nation together, but steely and uncompromising in defending two principles: no extension of slavery and no right to leave the Union. Lincoln's moral framework and the courage to stick to his beliefs enabled him to chart a clear course in the most perilous and chaotic time of a young nation.

CONVICTION AND COMMITMENT

Circumstances and personal inclinations push leaders toward one warrior role or another. Leaders need to be aware that they have choices with significant consequences. Adopting the role of the toxic warrior usually does more harm than good. Relentless warriors typically do more good than harm, but they pay a high price because their zest for combat encourages them to fight too hard or too recklessly. Principled warriors are particularly likely to alter the course of history. They leave a legacy for several reasons:

1. *Principled warriors put combat in perspective because they are not in love with it.*

Principled warriors bring courage, tenacity, and intensity, but unlike their toxic and relentless counterparts, they are committed to an overarching purpose rather than to power, self-aggrandizement, or running roughshod over opponents.

2. *Principled warriors will sacrifice for a worthy cause.*

General George Marshall, often viewed as the architect of victory in World War II, deferred without complaint to President Roosevelt's desire to keep him in Washington rather than sending him to command Allied forces in Europe. Marshall and Roosevelt both foresaw

the result: Eisenhower rather than Marshall would be remembered
as the general who bested Hitler. The same kind of commitment
defined Nelson Mandela. Facing a likely death sentence, he told a
South African court, "During my lifetime I have dedicated myself to
the struggle of the African people. I have fought against white domination, and I have fought against black domination. I have cherished
the ideal of a democratic and free society in which all persons live
together in harmony and with equal opportunities. It is an ideal
which I hope to live for and to achieve. But, if needs be, it is an ideal
for which I am prepared to die."[57]

Mandela, like Lincoln, Marshall, and many other principled warriors, hated war and violence, but would undertake whatever struggle
the higher cause required. He demonstrated during many years in
prison that he would pay any price and persevere for as long as it took.

3. *Commitment to a coherent set of purposes and values makes principled*
   warriors most likely to make a just and lasting difference.

Clarity of purpose keeps principled warriors focused on the big picture. It helps them avoid detours and chart a consistent course, while
it permits them to be flexible about strategies and tactics. With their
eyes on the prize, conviction and commitment fuel their determination
to pursue victory courageously and tirelessly. They are the warriors
most likely to be remembered far more for what they built than for
what they destroyed.

PART THREE

THE WARRIOR PATH

Regardless of the role they play, warriors succeed through a combination of four basic ingredients: heart, mind, skill, and weapons. *Heart* gives warriors passion, courage, and persistence—it is the "fire in the belly"—that propels them forward in the face of risk, confusion, danger, and obstacles. *Mind* gives warriors the direction and guidance to make strategic moves on life's ever-changing chessboard, avoiding snares, ambushes, and blind alleys. *Skill*—developed through instruction and experience—determines how well leaders read and manage people and circumstances to move their cause forward. *Weapons* are the armory

warrior leaders employ to champion their cause. Each of these ingredients contributes to the potential path to victory: overcoming a less determined or more fearful opponent with greater courage and passion, out-
smarting a more confused or less disciplined opponent with a better
game plan, besting an opponent through greater art and technique, or
winning by deploying stronger assets on the field—a larger force, better
players, or superior weaponry. The table at the end of this section summarizes these qualities, which are elaborated in the coming chapters.

*W*e see these warrior elements at play in the successful
career of Wal-Mart founder Sam Walton. When he took
over his first store in 1945—a struggling Ben Franklin
Variety Store in rural Arkansas—retail was already a mature industry in
the United States. The crowded and intensely competitive field included
big national players like Sears, Woolworth's, and J.C. Penney's, along
with thousands of regional and local outlets across the country. How
could the new owner of the second-best variety store in little New-
port, Arkansas, build the largest retail chain in the world? What kind
of knowledge or know-how did Walton, twenty-seven years old at
the time, possess that older and more experienced retailers lacked?

The answer lies in the unique combination of heart, mind, skill,
and weapons that Walton gradually accumulated. His *warrior heart*
showed up early in life—he always liked people, but he enjoyed winning even more. When he was an undergraduate at the University of
Missouri, his friends joked that he joined almost every club on cam-
pus just so he could run for office. He often won. He was also bitten
by the entrepreneurial bug early on. In college, he built a newspaper
delivery business that was so profitable his earnings were comparable
to those of many successful middle managers. After college, he con-
templated going to business school, but decided the benefits might
not justify the cost. He took a job with J.C. Penney's instead and fell
in love with retailing.[58]

HOW WARRIORS WIN

WARRIOR QUALITIES	ELEMENTS
Heart	Passion
	Courage
	Persistence
Mind	Knowing what you want
	Mapping the terrain and developing a game plan
	Responding adroitly to threats and opportunities
	Aligning passion to purpose
	Choosing your battles
Skill	Knowing the psyche
	Making friends and enlisting allies
	Rallying the troops
	Enlisting friends and buying off enemies
Weapons	Position
	Organization
	Allies
	Resources

Walton had a warrior's *mind.* In a brutal, cutthroat business, he bested his competitors with a simple but powerful game plan—cut costs, sell for less, offer a money-back guarantee, and go where your competitors aren't. His passion led him to work harder, travel more, and spend as much time as possible scouting competitors' stores

ing for any idea he could steal. His game plan provided direction and focus. An associate described him as "an old yard rooster who is rough, loves a good fight, and protects his territory."[59]

Walton also brought distinctive leadership *skills* that complemented his heart and intelligence. He was an astute judge of people, which helped him read customers, outfox competitors, raise capital, and recruit talent. Even as his company grew, he retained his common touch—visiting stores, talking to customers and sales clerks, and asking for their ideas and suggestions. That homey touch helped Walton convey a positive, almost warm and fuzzy image to most Wal-Mart consumers. It was an image that lingered after Walton's death.

6

WARRIOR HEART

Whatever course you decide upon, there is always someone to tell you you are wrong. There are always difficulties arising which tempt you to believe that your critics are right. To map out a course of action and follow it to the end, requires some of the same courage a soldier needs. Peace has its victories, but it takes brave men to win them.

—RALPH WALDO EMERSON[60]

No one plays to lose, but not everyone plays hard enough to win. In every arena of human conflict, there are countless examples of individuals or groups who beat an otherwise-superior opponent by dint of a bolder heart and steelier determination. Heart drives a leader's intensity and commitment; it is the wellspring for the passion, courage, and persistence that are crucial to success.

1. *Passion.*

Passion is at the heart of all successful leadership. It is rooted in a deep, sometimes obsessive, personal and emotional commitment to a cause, a group, or a task. It is a basic quality of all great warriors and leaders. It supplies energy, sustains courage, and fuels persistence. It is also contagious—the leader's passion, or lack of it, is felt by those who choose to follow.

2. *Courage.*

Courage is derived from the Latin word for heart. It is vital because conflict always brings risk of loss—physical, economic, or social. Leaders who lack courage run scared. They focus more on what could go wrong than on what might succeed. They succeed only when the going is smooth and risks are minimal. Leaders need an uncommon form of courage. It is easier to be brave if your job description requires it, you are following orders, or your teammates are urging you on. That is the courage of followers.

Leaders need a willingness to go beyond orders and job descriptions, to buck the tide and plunge into uncertain, dangerous waters. Sam Walton had that kind of courage. So did Joan of Arc, a young peasant girl who at age seventeen presented herself to the French court with the audacious claim that God had sent her to save France from the English. Almost everyone initially thought the girl must be crazy, but her passion and courage propelled her forward in the face of widespread doubt and formidable obstacles.

One of America's greatest military leaders, General George C. Marshall—architect of Allied victory in World War II and of the postwar Marshall Plan aiding Europe—showed a similar courage throughout his career. As a young major serving in France during World War I, he had the nerve to publicly confront the U.S. supreme commander, General Pershing, during an inspection tour:

> Pershing became unhappy with the level of training in the division and criticized the division commander in front of his subordinates.

Loyal to his commander and convinced the humiliation was unjustified, Marshall rose to his defense. When Pershing tried to ignore his protests and depart, Marshall exploded, placing his hand on Pershing's arm to prevent him from leaving and, according to Marshall's own recollections, practically forcing the general to listen.[61]

Marshall rubbed salt in the wound by adding that the real source of the problems was Pershing's headquarters. Marshall's colleagues, sure that he had committed career suicide, expressed their condolences. His fellow officers might have been dauntless in battle, but they found it hard to imagine showing so much courage in the face of a superior officer.

It turned out that they had misjudged both Marshall and Pershing. Respecting Marshall's candor, the general promoted him to colonel and added him to his own staff. More than two decades later, Marshall displayed the same bluntness in his first meeting with President Franklin D. Roosevelt. After Roosevelt presented his plan for averting U.S. involvement in World War II, he received reassuring nods from almost everyone in the room. To make it unanimous, the President turned to Marshall and said, "Don't you think so, George?" Marshall didn't think so and didn't like to be called George. He told Roosevelt as much. Roosevelt seemed startled, and the meeting ended abruptly. Once again those around him believed that Marshall was doomed. But Marshall earned the president's respect and became the military leader Roosevelt trusted most. As noted earlier, Marshall paid a price in the annals of history for Roosevelt's confidence. The president agonized over the decision, but reluctantly concluded he needed Marshall in Washington to oversee the war effort and could not afford to send him to Europe. But Marshall's courage was selfless rather than self-aggrandizing. He never uttered a word of complaint or regret.

3. *Persistence.*

Victory rarely comes quickly or easily. More often it is a long, costly, sometimes disheartening slog. Leaders are criticized when they are right and lacerated when they are wrong. Even the best leaders make mistakes and suffer defeats. They must often overcome doubt and fear in their friends and hatred from their foes. It is easy to become discouraged and to conclude that the game is no longer worth the effort. That is often fatal, as Clausewitz stated firmly more than a century ago:

> Perseverance in the chosen course is the essential counter-weight, provided that no compelling reasons intervene to the contrary. Moreover, there is hardly a worthwhile enterprise in war whose execution does not call for infinite effort, trouble, and privation; and as man under pressure tends to give in to physical and intellectual weakness, only great strength of will can lead to the objective. It is steadfastness that will earn the admiration of the world and of posterity.[62]

President Lincoln, already prone to depression, had many dark moments in the early years of the Civil War. He watched in despair as the Union army slouched from one costly defeat to another, each taking a horrendous toll in young lives. But his passion and courage sustained him and enabled him to persist until victory could finally be won.

After his team won a third Super Bowl in 2005, New England Patriots Coach Bill Belichick was hailed as one of the greatest coaches in the history of professional football. But five years earlier, Belichick had been fired from his first job as a head coach after five mostly dismal seasons in Cleveland. Many of the experts wondered what the Patriots were thinking when they hired Belichick as their new coach. Few predicted that his persistence through years of adversity had finally put him on the road to be hailed as a football genius.

Passion, courage, and persistence stoke the fire in the hearts of great leaders. Passion flows from a fierce commitment to a cause and to the people who will make it happen. Passion and conviction, in turn, kindle the courage and persistence that warrior leaders need to persevere in the face of the risks, danger, and discouragements that they will inevitably encounter.

7

WARRIOR MIND

The general who wins a battle makes many calculations in his temple ere the battle is fought. The general who loses a battle makes but few calculations beforehand. Thus do many calculations lead to victory and few calculations to defeat: how much more no calculation at all! It is by attention to this point that I can foresee who is likely to win or lose.

—SUN TZU[63]

Sun Tzu's point—made 2,500 years ago—still holds today. Heart sustains the warrior but may run amok if cut off from mind's direction and discipline. Mind without heart is sterile, but heart without mind is reckless, often suicidal. An effective leader needs both. Being smarter than your adversaries gives you a substantial edge. If you know the playing field better than your opponents and know more about them than they do about you, the odds shift in your favor. Great warrior leaders show consistent habits of mind.

1. *Focus: Knowing what you want.*

The first, the supreme, the most far-reaching act of judgment that the statesman and commander have to make is to establish the kind of war on which they are embarking; neither mistaking it for, nor trying to turn it into, something that is alien to its nature. This is the first of all strategic questions and the most comprehensive.

—CARL VON CLAUSEWITZ[64]

Clausewitz's principle seems obvious: never go into combat without knowing what you are fighting for and what price you are willing to pay. Clear thinking is never more important than before you embark on a campaign. Yet this principle is regularly violated, often with tragic results. Leaders overreact to immediate pressures and provocations, allowing passion or truncated judgment to lead them into a terrible dilemma—they cannot afford to lose, yet the price of victory is more than they can pay. U.S. Secretary of State Colin Powell, a veteran warrior, was well aware of this when he warned President George W. Bush about the risks of invading Iraq: "If you break it, you will own it." Subsequent events confirmed the wisdom of Powell's counsel. The costs of the U.S. occupation turned out to be far higher than predicted, and success became hard to define and harder to achieve. But once in, there was no easy way out.

2. *Foresight: Mapping the terrain and developing a game plan.*

Once your purpose is clear, you need a game plan: a detailed map from here to there. There is truth in the adage that plans rarely survive the first contact with the enemy. But that makes it even more important to have a strategy going in. It is foolhardy to plunge into a minefield without knowing where explosives are buried, yet leaders unwittingly do it all the time. They launch new initiatives before they have a good grasp of the theater of battle. In any competitive arena, if you think harder and better than your opponents, you will probably win.

At minimum, a good map needs to take account of the local terrain and the players. In his classic treatise on strategy, Sun Tzu devoted three chapters to analysis of terrain, identifying criteria for assessing whether a location is favorable or unfavorable. One criterion is ease of entry—if you try to enter a particular market or arena, will you encounter obstacles such as well-entrenched opponents? A second test is ease of exit: once in, how hard will it be to get out? A third yardstick is whether you will be on high, level, or low ground—are you likely to be at an advantage or a disadvantage. Avoid bad ground. Fight where the odds are in your favor.

As important as knowing the terrain is understanding the individuals, groups, or organizations who will be playing with you. Two key characteristics of any player are interests (what the player wants) and power (how much influence and control the player is capable of exerting). Players' interests determine what is at stake, and whether they are likely to be allies, opponents, or fence-sitters. Players' power determines how much they can help or hinder your cause. Different players require different approaches. You improve your odds by mobilizing allies, tilting fence-sitters in your direction, and neutralizing opponents. If your allies are active and your opponents stay on the sidelines, you're in good shape. If the opposite is true, your prospects are poor.

The dynamics of conflict are often very fluid, so that the map you develop today may change significantly tomorrow. An effective game plan has to build in flexibility and contingencies. Every warrior encounters change and surprise. Winners handle it better. As a leader you will often face intelligent and resourceful opponents who will do their best to frustrate your intentions and exploit weaknesses in your strategy. The better you prepare for what your opponents might do, the less likely you are to be caught off guard and suffer defeat.

3. *Flexibility: Responding fluidly to threats and opportunities.*

"Throwing good money after bad" is one metaphor for the process of self-entrapment—clinging stubbornly to a course of action long after it has stopped making sense. Within a few months after the Allied invasion of Europe on D-Day in June 1944, it was clear that only two questions remained about Germany's defeat: How long? and At what price? On the western front, it was a face-off between Dwight Eisenhower and Adolph Hitler. One of Eisenhower's advantages was that he and his team were more flexible warriors than Germany's Führer. Confident in the generals who reported to him, Eisenhower gave them broad leeway to experiment and improvise. Hitler took the opposite tack. Blaming his commanders for Germany's deteriorating fortunes, Hitler believed that he alone had the vision and will to achieve victory. He listened less and less to his generals and insisted on making all major decisions, even though he was increasingly remote from military reality.

> Flexibility was Eisenhower's outstanding tactical quality. He never allowed his mind to become set or rigid. He was usually successful at creating tactical situations with a number of alternatives. This in turn allowed him to exploit any lucky break. Flexibility set him apart from most planners, including his own G-3 [operations and training section]. One never knew what to expect in war, except that the unexpected was likely. Only those who were ready could take advantage of the breaks, and to be ready it was imperative to have reserves.[65]

Mao Zedong, another wily and successful warrior, also emphasized the importance of flexibility in battle: "Skill in conducting guerrilla operations, however, lies not in merely understanding the things we have discussed but rather in their actual application on the field of battle. The quick intelligence that constantly watches the ever-changing situation and is able to seize on the right moment for decisive action is found only in keen and thoughtful observers."[66]

4. *Discipline: Aligning passion with purpose.*

Passion in leaders and warriors is double-edged—vital but dangerous. Combat and conflict trigger powerful, sometimes overwhelming, emotions—among them rage, resentment, humiliation, terror, shame, and vengefulness. All can be potent sources of energy and motivation, but unchecked, they can easily lead to ruin. Thomas Edison was an extraordinary genius whose inventive mind produced the light bulb, the phonograph, and the movie camera. But he could be as stubborn when wrong as when he was right. The clearest case in point was Edison's conviction that the future of the electric industry lay in DC (direct current) rather than AC (alternating current). AC, he felt, was too dangerous. He discounted the importance of DC's great competitive flaw—it couldn't be transmitted very far. When his closest rival, George Westinghouse, took up the AC cause, Edison launched the "war of the currents." He "used every means fair or foul to thwart Westinghouse and his supporters, including the charge that they were foisting a lethal technology upon an unwary public. It proved an ugly fight, but in the end Edison's DC was no match for a system that could transmit current hundreds of miles compared to mere city blocks."[67]

Another famous example of stubbornness in the face of opposition comes from the 1950s, near the end of IBM founder Tom Watson Sr.'s career. Watson was highly successful as both warrior and wizard (as discussed in Chapter Sixteen), but he began to outlive his usefulness near the end of his reign as IBM's chief executive. The aging patriarch engaged in constant battles with his son, Tom Watson Jr., to whom he was gradually but grudgingly turning over control of his company. Their last great battle was over a government antitrust suit. Junior wanted to sign a consent agreement and move on, but his father was still aggrieved by the jail sentence he'd received (though never served) for restraint-of-trade violations more than thirty years earlier. Watson Sr. dug in and battled the Justice Department for five years. He only relented a few months before his death.

His son was finally able to settle, but on terms that were substantially worse than IBM could have obtained years earlier.[68]

5. *Discretion: Choosing your battles.*

Never fight against heavy odds, if by any possible maneuvering you can hurl your own force on only a part, and that the weakest part, of your enemy and crush it. Such tactics will win every time, and a small army may thus destroy a large one in detail, and repeated victory will make it invincible.

—STONEWALL JACKSON[69]

In guerrilla warfare, select the tactic of seeming to come from the east and attacking from the west; avoid the solid, attack the hollow; attack; withdraw; deliver a lightning blow, seek a lightning decision. When guerrillas engage a stronger enemy, they withdraw when he advances; harass him when he stops; strike him when he is weary; pursue him when he withdraws. In guerilla strategy, the enemy's rear, flanks, and other vulnerable spots are his vital points, and there he must be harassed, attacked, dispersed, exhausted and annihilated.

—MAO ZEDONG[70]

Jackson and Mao lived in very different cultures and historical circumstances, but they agreed on a tenet of wise warriors. Choosing your battles is corollary to the principle of subordinating passion to purpose. If you fight because of anger, revenge, or a need to prove yourself, you will often act foolishly. This violates what Mao called the fundamental axiom of all combat: conserve your strength, destroy the enemy's strength.

In 1913, Theodore Vail (long-time leader of AT&T) found himself facing possible antitrust action in the wake of his company's purchase of Western Union. Vail disliked antitrust suits as much as his friend Tom Watson did, but he coolly chose discretion over valor.

Believing the battle not worth fighting, he sent representatives to Washington to work out a deal. The eventual agreement required AT&T to divest Western Union and to let the six thousand independent phone companies across America interconnect with AT&T's long distance lines. Vail averted a battle he expected to lose; the press gave him credit for being a responsible corporate citizen. More important, the deal freed him to pursue his goal of making "Ma Bell" a quasi-monopoly. The interconnection agreement strengthened AT&T's position as the dominant long distance carrier in the United States. Most important, nothing in the agreement hindered the company from continuing to buy up smaller phone companies. Vail won more than he lost by avoiding a fight. AT&T eventually controlled more than 80 percent of U.S. telephones, and the Bell system became the world's largest and richest company. It was finally broken up by another antitrust suit more than half a century after Vail's death.[71]

HABITS OF MIND

Heart propels, but mind must guide the warrior leader. Passion absent intelligence has led countless warriors into reckless, foolish, and self-destructive actions. Leaders must begin with focus—a clear sense of what they want. Next they need foresight, the ability to map the terrain of battle and develop a game plan. But no plan anticipates all the contingencies of conflict, so warriors also need flexibility to change course in the light of new circumstances. A fourth component of warrior mind is discipline—the art of aligning passion with purpose. Discipline in turn makes discretion possible—the ability to choose your battles and fight only when the time and circumstances favor your cause.

8

WARRIOR SKILL

Skills are capacities developed over time. Genes confer potential, but potential becomes usable skill only through effort, practice, and instruction.

*T*he skills warriors need depend on where and how they fight. Historically, skill in using a sword or a rifle was essential. For the modern leader, the most important skills are personal and psychological, variations on the theme of emotional intelligence.[72] Leaders need to know how to read people and recruit them to their cause. They need ability to motivate and inspire allies and followers. They must learn to negotiate with friends for support and with enemies for workable pacts. In this chapter, we discuss four key skills: intuition, recruiting, inspiration, and bargaining.

1. *Intuition: Knowing the psyche.*

If you know the enemy and know yourself, you need not fear the result of a hundred battles. If you know yourself but not the enemy, for every victory gained you will also suffer a defeat. If you know neither the enemy nor yourself, you will succumb in every battle.

—SUN TZU[73]

The route to victory gets smoother the more you can develop confidence and conviction among your allies while sowing lethargy, confusion, fear or, even better, respect and affection among your opponents. To do this, great leaders have to be great students of the psyche, expert in understanding and managing hopes and fears of both supporters and opponents. One of our greatest presidents, Abraham Lincoln, a fictional mob boss, Don Vito Corleone, and a great entrepreneur, Mary Kay Ash, had one thing in common—all were master students of psychology.

In Mario Puzo's classic novel (and academy award–winning film), *The Godfather,* Don Vito Corleone has become one of the most powerful men in America as the head of his sprawling Mafia family. One key to his success is his ability to read and manipulate everyone around him. He flatters, supports, and ingratiates himself to friends and allies. He manipulates, terrorizes, and if necessary eliminates opponents. His manner is almost invariably warm and ingratiating.

He never raises his voice, loses his temper, or makes idle threats. Yet his ability to make offers people can't refuse enables him to get what he wants.

When he became president in 1860, Abraham Lincoln needed similar skills to forge a cabinet out of a group of political enemies, including his three principal rivals for the Republican presidential nomination.[74] One of them, Senator William H. Seward of New York, had grumbled that he was "justly entitled to the Republican nomination for the presidency, and . . . had to stand aside and see it given to a little Illinois lawyer."[75] Another, Senator Salmon P. Chase of Ohio, had long been a passionate leader in the antislavery movement. Lincoln won the nomination primarily because he had made fewer enemies than the other leading candidates.

A less secure man than Lincoln would have filled his cabinet with people he was sure he could trust and control. But Lincoln made Seward Secretary of State, and Chase Secretary of the Treasury, even though each had made it clear that he had no desire to be in a cabinet with the other. Lincoln wanted them as members of his team rather than critics on Capitol Hill. Told "they will eat you up," Lincoln responded, "They will be just as likely to eat each other up."[76]

Lincoln's strategy was tested early and often. A month after joining the cabinet, Seward sent Lincoln a memorandum saying in effect that Lincoln was aimless and incompetent but that Seward was willing to fill in the deficiencies.[77] Instead of attacking Seward or demanding his resignation, Lincoln calmly replied that he intended to continue doing the president's job himself. Over the next few trying years, Lincoln was able to keep his fractious team of powerful and self-important men together only because of his personal skills and his insight into their psyches.

Mary Kay Ash, the founder of May Kay Cosmetics, built her successful direct sales business with a passionate focus on the needs and aspirations of women who were frustrated with their lives and their careers. She knew they wanted income. But they also wanted to feel better about themselves and be more in control of their lives.

As Ash put it, "I feel that God has led me into this position to help women to know how great they really are."[78] Beloved by thousands of grateful women, Mary Kay Ash had another, much tougher side. She fought back ferociously when competitors invaded her turf, referring to the head of one rival firm as the Leona Helmsley of the cosmetics business. CBS reporter Morley Safer described Ash as a "pink panther whose instinct for doing business and making money is as finely tuned as a jungle cat going for the kill."[79]

2. Recruiting: Making friends and enlisting allies.

In combat, you want comrades at your side, and they need a reason to support you. To gain their loyalty, you need to cultivate relationships and offer compelling reasons to join your team.

Skills in recruiting help you do that. Recruiting skill is partly related to personal qualities like charm, charisma, energy, and attractiveness. Such characteristics enable some individuals to light up a room and attract others magnetically. Ronald Reagan had those qualities in abundance, while his immediate predecessors, Gerald Ford and Jimmy Carter, were less gifted. *Charisma* derives from a Greek word for "gift," and may be to a large degree a quality that people are (or aren't) born with. But one component of recruiting, horse trading, is a skill that can be learned and polished. Legendary legislative leaders like Thomas P. "Tip" O'Neill and Lyndon Johnson developed this skill to a fine art. A recent Congressional exemplar is Republican House Majority Leader Tom DeLay, arguably the most powerful member of Congress during the administration of President George W. Bush. When indictments over alleged ethical lapses threatened to engulf DeLay in 2005, his fellow Republicans showed remarkable willingness to stand by their man:

> The reason, it seems, is that over the years, brick by brick, Mr. DeLay has built a wall of political support. His small acts of kindness have become lore. Pizza during late night votes. Travel arrangements for low-level lawmakers. Birthday wishes, get-well cards,

condolences for House members in emotional need. On a larger scale, friends—and enemies—describe him as a favor-trader extraordinaire, piling up a mountain of goodwill. Almost every Republican in the House owes Mr. DeLay for something—a job, a piece of legislation or a large campaign contribution.[80]

One colleague described DeLay as an extraordinary psychologist with a keen understanding of "what makes members tick and what makes them successful. Tom knows every member's district, he knows their needs politically, he knows their interests, he almost always understands their family situations."[81] But DeLay's skills were not limited to pizza and favors. He understood the importance of being feared as well as liked, and was just as skilled at punishing enemies as at doing favors for friends. He provides a modern-day portrait of President Lyndon Johnson's legendary applications of the carrot and the stick to get his way.

3. *Inspiration: Rallying the troops.*

Winning requires a highly motivated, spirited team. Sometimes followers will be so zealous that you need only stand out of their way. More often, you need to pump up the troops on a regular basis. Knowing the psyche is vital: rallying your constituents is essentially the art of making an offer so attractive they can't wait to sign up. The offer needs to respond to their desire to be part of something bigger as well as cater to more immediate, personal concerns.

The film *Patton* opens with a dramatic scene in which General Patton, framed by an immense American flag, gears up his soldiers on the eve of battle. The flag was Hollywood hyperbole, but the content of the speech was mostly accurate—except that filmmakers toned down some of the general's more pungent phrases. Patton was uniquely gifted in the use of profanity, believing it was a vital tool for reaching troops. "It may not sound nice to a bunch of little old ladies at a tea party, but it helps my soldiers to remember. You can't run an army without profanity," he once said, "and it has to be eloquent profanity. An army without profanity couldn't fight its way out of a piss-soaked paper bag."[82] This philosophy was evident from beginning to end in the movie version of the speech; the original was delivered in England in June 1944 on the eve of D-Day. After an introduction by a fellow general, Patton strode to the platform, resplendent in polished boots and pearl-handled revolver. He meticulously inspected the honor guard, surveyed the expectant crowd, and began his speech:

Men, this stuff that some sources sling around about America wanting out of this war, not wanting to fight, is a crock of bullshit. Americans love to fight, traditionally. All real Americans love the sting and clash of battle. You are here today for three reasons. First, because you are here to defend your homes and your loved ones. Second, you are here for your own self-respect, because you would not want to be anywhere else. Third, you are here because you are real men and all real men like to fight. When you, here, every one of you, were kids, you all admired the champion marble player, the fastest runner, the toughest boxer, the big league ball players, and the All-American football players. Americans love a winner. Americans will not tolerate a loser. Americans despise cowards. Americans play to win all of the time. I wouldn't give a hoot in hell for a man who lost and laughed. That's why Americans have never lost nor will ever lose a war; for the very idea of losing is hateful to an American.[83]

Patton's opening immediately offered answers to three vital questions. First: What is the larger purpose of the enterprise; what are we here to do? The second is the personal meaning for each individual: What's in it for me, and what is my role? Third: Will we succeed? Later in the speech, he directly addressed a concern that haunted his audience—the fear of dying in battle:

Death, in time, comes to all men. Yes, every man is scared in his first battle. If he says he's not, he's a liar. Some men are cowards but they fight the same as the brave men or they get the hell slammed out of them watching men fight who are just as scared as they are. The real hero is the man who fights even though he is scared.[84]

In his conclusion, Patton used verbal sleight-of-hand to leave his audience with an image of hope:

The General paused. His eagle like eyes swept over the hillside. He said with pride, "There is one great thing that you men will all be able to say after this war is over and you are home once again. You may be thankful that twenty years from now when you are sitting by the fireplace with your grandson on your knee, and he asks you what you did in the great World War II, you WON'T have to cough, shift him to the other knee and say, "Well, your Granddaddy shoveled shit in Louisiana."[85]

Patton had acknowledged earlier that some men would die, but his closing lines offered a rhetorical promise that every soldier would live to become a hero in the eyes of his grandson.

Patton's speech might fail with other audiences or other occasions, but his message was attuned to his listeners. He knew they were young, untried, and terrified. He knew they needed to be bucked up and reassured about the importance of the mission. He also knew that deep down they wanted to be heroes. He knew their fears and their hopes better than they did and gave them what they wanted. They responded with laughter, enthusiasm, and thunderous applause.

4. *Bargaining: Enlisting friends and buying off enemies.*

J. P. Morgan, builder of one of America's greatest banking houses, dominated American finance for decades in the nineteenth and early twentieth centuries. He became so powerful that two U.S. presidents called on him to bail the country out of financial crises. He did it both times—at a profit. He was feared in some quarters and despised in others as an exemplar of the worst evils of capitalism.[86] How to explain, then, that a man as tough and smart as Morgan sometimes chose to leave money on the table in negotiations? In 1873, when Morgan and fellow tycoon Andrew Carnegie were still relatively early in their careers, Carnegie hit a crunch that left him desperate for cash. Morgan offered to buy Carnegie's share of a partnership the two of them owned jointly. Carnegie said he would gladly sell for a partnership credit of $50,000, plus $10,000 for profit. Morgan agreed. But when Carnegie called on Morgan the next day to get his cash, Morgan gave him two checks: one for $60,000, and one for $10,000. Carnegie was surprised, but Morgan explained that Carnegie had underestimated the credit he was owed by $10,000. "Well that is something worthy of you," said Carnegie as he tried to give back the extra $10,000.[87] Morgan would not take it. Carnegie never forgot, and always saw Morgan as someone he could trust.

Some three decades later, as Carnegie was contemplating retirement, Morgan maneuvered to buy his steel business, and arranged for one of Carnegie's closest associates to raise the issue on the golf course. After brief reflection, Carnegie scribbled a price of $480 million on a piece of paper. It was a breathtaking sum at the time, enough to make Carnegie arguably the world's richest man. Morgan accepted the price immediately. He trusted Carnegie, and he knew that Carnegie trusted him.

A few years later, Carnegie said to Morgan, "I made one mistake, Pierpont, when I sold out to you."

"What was that?" inquired Morgan.

"I should have asked you for a hundred million more than I did.

"You would have got it if you had."[88]

Bargaining is a process of making deals that work for all parties concerned. Morgan was a wise warrior who understood that every transaction has both short- and long-term implications. In the short term, it resolves immediate interests. But in the longer term it can also build relationships and achieve one of the warrior's most important needs—creating allies rather than opponents.

A fundamental dilemma in negotiations is choosing between win-win and win-lose. Should you collaborate with other parties to try to make the pie bigger? Or focus on getting the biggest possible piece for yourself?

One of the best-known win-win approaches to negotiation was developed by Roger Fisher and William Ury in *Getting to Yes.* They argue that bargainers lose the forest for the trees—they are so focused on getting a bigger share that they miss opportunities to make everyone better off. Fisher and Ury propose a win-win approach called "principled bargaining," built around four strategies. The first strategy is to "separate the people from the problem." Be tough on the issues, but treat other parties with respect. The second rule of thumb is to "focus on interests, not positions."[89] J. P. Morgan's decision to volunteer an extra $10,000 to Andrew Carnegie recognized just this point. Carnegie would have been entirely happy with his initial request for $60,000. But Morgan saw a long-term interest in building Carnegie's trust. Morgan invested $10,000. Years later he got a $100 million payoff.

Fisher and Ury's third recommendation is to invent options for mutual gain—looking for new possibilities that bring advantages to both sides. Parties often lock on to the first alternatives that come to mind and stop searching. Generating more options increases the chance of better decisions. Fisher and Ury's fourth strategy is to "insist on objective criteria"—standards of fairness for both substance and procedures. A classic example of fair procedure involves the old standby for dividing any pie (real or metaphorical): one claimant makes up the portions, and the other chooses whichever seems preferable.

Fisher and Ury recommend concentrating on better solutions for both parties rather than on the best deal for yourself. Others disagree, citing many examples in which shrewd, self-interested negotiators have achieved great victories. Bill Gates offered to license an operating system to IBM in 1980 about forty-eight hours before he had one. Meanwhile, he pointedly did not tell Tim Paterson of Seattle Computer that Microsoft was buying his operating system to resell it to IBM. Microsoft gave IBM a great price: only $30,000 more than the $50,000 they'd paid for it. But Gates shrewdly retained the rights to license it to anyone else. Within a year, Microsoft had licensed MS-DOS to fifty companies, and the number kept growing.[90] Onlookers who wondered why Microsoft was so aggressive and unyielding in battling the Justice Department's antitrust suit twenty years later might not have known that Gates had been a dogged adherent of win-lose bargaining for a long time.

Expanding the pie and claiming the best piece you can get are both central to the bargaining process. How does a leader decide how to balance the two? At least two questions are important: How much opportunity is there for a win-win solution? and How important are long-term relationships with these people? If an agreement can make everyone better off, it makes sense to emphasize creating value. If you expect to work with the same people in the future, as Morgan did with Carnegie, it is often shortsighted to use value-claiming tactics that leave anger and mistrust in their wake.

SKILL MATTERS

Four skills are critical for warrior leaders. They need *intuition* to read the thinking and intentions of both friends and enemies, so as to predict what others are likely to do and know how best to influence them. *Recruiting* skills enable them to sign people up to their cause, and *inspiration* gives them the ability to motivate and fire up the troops after they have signed up. Finally, *bargaining* skills enable them to negotiate favorable deals with allies and opponents alike.

9

WARRIOR WEAPONS

I always make it a rule to get there first with the most men.

—GENERAL NATHAN BEDFORD FORREST[91]

No warrior wants to go into battle unarmed. Weapons translate heart, mind, and skill into power. Historically, weapons were physical implements of combat—swords, lances, rifles, and the like. Warriors carried and wielded them with their own hands. Such weapons still exist and are vital in some circumstances. But the most important tools of the warrior leader are not physical but social, economic, and institutional.

*I*n both film and novel, Mario Puzo's *The Godfather* opens with a wedding reception for Don Vito Corleone's daughter. Following tradition, the Don holds court as friends and retainers come to pledge their friendship and loyalty. Some also come to ask his assistance on some problem they believe only he can solve. They know he will feel particularly obliged to help them on this special day. Trust in his powers is so strong that a dying friend pleads in all seriousness for the Don to intercede with God on his behalf. The Don disclaims a direct channel to the Almighty, but obliges whenever he can, because loyal friends and allies are a vital source of his power. Personally, the Don possesses many of the skills of a warrior leader discussed in the preceding chapter. Those skills enabled him to assemble a formidable array of weapons—his allies, his position as the head of a Mafia family, the family's capabilities, and the resources that he controls either directly or indirectly—that were the building blocks of his power. Weapons are the fourth essential element in a warrior leader's success.

1. *Position.*

Where you are situated is often more important than who you are in determining how much power you can exert. Generals have more power than colonels, who outrank privates. More powerful and visible roles provide at least three key power sources:

- *Authority:* The right to make decisions that are binding on those within the scope of your office.

- *Access:* Ability to get the ear of key decision makers and to get a seat at the table when important decisions are made.

- *Visibility:* The "bully pulpit" that makes it easier to get people's attention and make your point.

Positions that carry high levels of authority, access, and visibility come with burdens as well—responsibilities, cross-pressures, and constraints—but leaders are usually willing to bear that price because powerful roles make it so much easier to get things done.

2. *Organization.*

It makes a big difference if you are fighting with or without an army. Organizations are created precisely because they are capable of doing things well beyond the capacity of any individual. They are tools—sometimes very powerful tools—in the hands of anyone who can control their complex dynamics. An organization's power depends on a number of factors, including its size, capabilities, resources, visibility, manageability, and environment. Larger organizations are typically more powerful than smaller ones, because they can do more things and have more resources and greater visibility. The "but" is that size makes large organizations more unwieldy. A fast and heroic horse may be priceless or useless, depending on whether you can ride it. When big organizations become ungovernable, they are often out-maneuvered by smaller, more nimble competitors.

Because organizations and their subunits vary greatly in terms of their capabilities, the group or organization you are in can be as important as your title, or more so.[92] Your position affects which of an organization's capacities you can use, but no organization can offer you means it does not possess. A backwater department or a mud-dled, failing organization may actually make you weaker by blocking or dissipating whatever power you have. In every professional sport, there are examples of great players who never win championships because fate puts them on weak teams. On the other side of the coin are the benchwarmers who wear championship rings because they were favored with great coaches and teammates. Even a bit part or minor job in a very powerful group can give you substantial visibility and clout. In the federal government, for example, even low-level staffers may have great power if they work at the White House. Their messages get read and their calls are returned because of their proximity to the president.

3. *Resources.*

You have power when you own or control things that other people want. Those assets may be tangible (like money or petroleum) or intangible (like access or prestige). They may be durable (like land) or evanescent (like tickets to a hot concert or sporting event). The important thing is how much others want what you control, and how much you can help or hinder them in getting what they want. The more you can do for them, the more they will do for you. Every four years, the 640,000 registered voters in the state of New Hampshire become the world's most powerful and coveted electorate for a brief period in February and March. Theirs is the first presidential primary, and it makes or breaks candidates every four years. New Hampshire's voters are a small and unrepresentative sample of the U.S. population, but they are powerful gatekeepers upon whom candidates shower time and money.

4. *Allies.*

The solitary warrior, a courageous and indomitable hero, is deeply rooted in legend, myth, and movies. The loner also plays a central role in many of the stories we read or watch. Whether your preferences run to Jackie Chan, Arnold Schwarzenegger, Vin Diesel, or Uma Thurman, there's an action hero for almost every taste, ethnicity, and gender. In film, one powerful individual often defeats an entire army, fulfilling a deep hope we all share: with skill, courage, and luck, one person can change the world. In the real world, solitary warriors usually lose, outnumbered and overwhelmed by opponents who mobilize a larger force. Smart leaders, like Anne Mulcahy when she became CEO of Xerox in August 2001, understand that they need friends and allies. At the time, few observers gave Mulcahy much chance of success:

> Xerox had $17.1 billion in debt and $154 million in cash. It was
> about to begin seven straight quarters of losses. The credit markets
> had slammed shut. An SEC investigation of the Mexico unit was

about to spread to other parts of the company. Reorganizations of the sales force and the billing centers had led to chaos. In 2000 the stock fell from $63.69 a share to $4.43, the company lost 90 percent of its market cap, and the best and brightest headed for the exits. The board had one last chance—and, boy, was she a long shot.[93]

Warren Buffett summarized her plight succinctly, "You didn't get promoted. You went to war." Yet three years later, *Business Week* put Mulcahy on its list of the best managers of 2004. The stock was up, the company was profitable again, and Mulcahy had met earnings targets ten quarters in a row. Mulcahy's success formula combined passion, hard work, and recognition from the beginning that she needed allies—lots of them, both inside and outside the company. "Constantly on the move, Mulcahy met with bankers, reassured customers, galvanized employees. She sometimes visited three cities a day."[94]

Her predecessor had been fired after only thirteen months on the job, partly as a result of "executive-suite discord so intractable as to amount to corporate civil war."[95] Mulcahy had no chance without a strong and loyal executive team. She met personally with more than a hundred top executives to sell them on the opportunities and determine if they were willing to be "all about Xerox." She met constantly with bankers and financial advisers and gradually, painstakingly convinced them that she and Xerox had a future they could afford to invest in.

Anne Mulcahy understood what many would-be leaders never fully appreciate. Position power is important, but it is never enough. Organizations and societies are networks as well as hierarchies, and the power of relationships is a crucial complement to the power of position. In simplest terms, network power amounts to the power of your friends minus the power of your enemies. Mulcahy understood the truth in the old advice to "keep your friends close and your enemies closer." She saw and acted on the need to rally friends while converting skeptics and enemies into allies whenever possible.

WEAPONS ARE VITAL

Weapons, the tools of combat, leverage the warrior leader's heart, mind, and skill. For warrior leaders, four assets are paramount: position, organization, resources, and allies. Powerful roles provide authority, visibility, and access to information. Your own army—a group or organization whose assets you can use—increases your odds on the field of combat. The same is true of allies, and of resources that can be used as bargaining chips to influence both allies and opponents.

Weapons are of little use unless a warrior knows why and how to use them, but they are a vital complement to other central attributes of warrior leaders. These leaders need heart to fire courage and passion. They need warrior mind to provide direction and discipline. They need skill—art, craft, and technique—to fight as well as their opponents, or better. With these four basic qualities—heart, mind, skill, and weapons—they are prepared to enter the arena.

PART FOUR

WIZARD ROLES

Authentic, Wannabe, and Harmful

Throughout history, people have been fascinated by the magical power of wizards and wizardry. Wizards are part of an ensemble of players who devote themselves to the mystical, symbolic aspects of a tribe or organization. Other related roles include sorcerer, magus, magician, and shaman. What sets wizards apart is captured in the root meaning, "wise."

*M*ost of us are acquainted with Merlin and Gandalf, wizards of a more or less fictional yesteryear. In legend these were magical people with supernatural powers. They could "turn cats into owls, produce lavish banquets with a wave of the wand, disappear into thin air, or cast spells to make castles look like cabbages."[96] Their mode of dress set them apart from normal people: long flowing robes, perhaps a conical hat adorned with the signs of the zodiac and other symbols. But their chief role was to offer sage advice: Merlin as a tutor and counselor to King Arthur; Gandalf through stories and wisdom in his itinerant travels throughout the countryside. Both were preoccupied with the future and confronting evil powers that might cast a dark shadow over their world's long-term prospects.

Our interest in wizards has endured into contemporary times. Through the Harry Potter series, J. K. Rowling has introduced us to Albus Dumbledore, the master of Hogwarts School and an extraordinary wizard whose magical powers rival those attributed to Merlin and Gandalf. But most of his magical deeds are reserved for practical purposes. His power as a wizard is often portrayed in hearsay and stories. Like his historical kin, Dumbledore seems to regard his key role as dispensing sound advice. But the advice is often cryptic, and he does not insist that it be followed. He wants people to think for themselves and learn from their mistakes. Like other wizards, he can predict the future only imperfectly, but his deep knowledge and keen intuition often enable him to make excellent forecasts.

What do magic and wizardry have to do with current conceptions of leadership? Not much, if we think of them as irrational fairy tales suitable only for the young or weak-minded. The closest we come to the more mystical side of leadership is in using the term *charisma* to explain why some leaders flourish and others falter or fall. The dictionary defines *charisma* as a gift of god's grace, a divinely inspired gift, talent, or grace that captures the imagination, allegiance, and devotion of others. O'Keefe simplifies this by defining magicians and wizards as "the literalists of the imagination."[97] These more modern versions of magic and wizards are embedded in historical and contemporary roots that the field of leadership has mostly neglected.

The phrase "the wizards of Langley," which describes the spymasters at the Central Intelligence Agency, implies that they have esoteric knowledge, unusual capacities and powers, and the ability to make things happen in mysterious ways. More broadly, the basic work of wizards is to create and transform. They use their imagination, insight, and wisdom to see beneath the surface and beyond the mundane. They see possibilities others miss and use powers others lack. In every realm of human enterprise, many of the leaders who have made a difference have been wizards. Like warriors, wizards can work in a variety of ways. How they lead and the impact they make varies according to the role they play.

In story and legend, we find numerous examples of three wizard archetypes, personified in the *Lord of the Rings* trilogy by Sauron, Gollum, and Gandalf. Sauron exemplifies the role of the *harmful wizard*—he is immensely powerful but long ago embraced the dark side of magic. Sauron seeks power and destruction. That is his only legacy. Gollum, a small, hunched figure obsessed by his desire to possess and wield great magic power, is a *wannabe wizard*. As is often true of wannabes, he flirts tantalizingly with success, without quite grasping the gold ring he seeks. Gandalf personifies the *authentic wizard*. Like Merlin and Dumbledore, he is an old man with wise face and long flowing beard. Gandalf's wisdom, more than anything else, is responsible for the evil Sauron's eventual downfall.

If we look for wizards among contemporary leaders and would-be leaders, we find many who play roles very similar to those of the mythic figures from *The Lord of the Rings*. The table at the end of this section provides contemporary examples from a number of different fields of endeavor.

Our goal is to revive the positive aspects of magic and wizardry, and to link them to the challenges a leader faces today. How does a leader create or transform an organization, relying heavily on symbols to produce both tangible and mystical results that capture people's imaginations and loyalty? How can a leader avoid the traps and resist the darker side of magic, which produces destruction instead of positive creation or transformation? We explore those questions in the next three chapters.

EXAMPLES OF WIZARD ROLES

LEADERSHIP POSITION	HARMFUL	WANNABE	AUTHENTIC
Business chief executives	Frank Lorenzo	Ken Lay	Liz Clayborne
Military leaders	Hermann Goering	William Westmoreland	Norman Schwarzkopf
American presidents	Warren Harding	Woodrow Wilson	Ronald Reagan
Basketball coaches	Dave Bliss	Rudy Tomjanovich	Phil Jackson

10

THE
AUTHENTIC
WIZARD

As with warriors, wizards come in many forms tagged with different labels: magician, alchemist, shaman, sorcerer, or witch. Regardless of label, they are people "who make things happen that shouldn't happen."[98] They work on a symbolic level, using myth, ritual, ceremony, and stories to shape people's attitudes and beliefs, thereby creating or transforming social patterns or ways. As Joseph Campbell observed, "It requires neither wealth nor machinery to invent a new trick, but only *an attitude of mind*—and this attitude, it now seems to me, is the real key to our achievement."[99]

*A*uthentic wizardry, as distinct from hucksterism or fraud, is especially relevant at a time when people distrust their leaders. In recent years, corporate scandals, moral turpitude in the clergy, misconduct by elected politicians, and ethical breaches by health care professionals have all chipped away at the public's faith and confidence, making people more reluctant to believe anything, no matter how attractive it appears on the surface. We have come to expect the worst behind alluring promises and flashy façades.

Authentic wizards have discovered their passion or calling through hard work and inner reflection. Their genuineness leads others to see them as real and worth joining in a common quest. The wizard's long-term vision may be hazy. But faith that a group is moving in a noble direction creates a sustaining spirit that encourages even jaundiced cynics to suspend disbelief temporarily and sign on with the enterprise. A job for pay becomes work toward something special.

Ronald Reagan and Franklin D. Roosevelt modeled authentic wizardry in the U.S. presidency. Both talked to America in ways that touched, comforted, and inspired. In business, Oprah Winfrey and the late Mary Kay Ash stand out for their ability to bring magic to the lives of their adoring fans. Political leaders like Colin Powell and John McCain radiate character and serve as emblems of American virtues. Medicine still can showcase clinicians like Dr. Paul Farmer, chronicled for his commitment to serving Haiti's poorest,[100] and Dr. Peter Minnich, a kidney transplant surgeon with a heart as well as a skilled set of hands. Both are more devoted to patient care than to the size of their practice or the thickness of their wallets.

Two authentic wizards, David Neeleman, CEO of JetBlue, and Thomas Keller, head chef of the French Laundry, demonstrate that a little magic can go a long way in creating virtuous enterprises in very different industries.

THE STORY OF JETBLUE

Deregulation hit the U.S. airline industry in 1978, and things have never been the same. The intent was to prune government regulation and open the skies to competition. Fifty-eight fledgling start-ups took the bait and cobbled together air service to a variety of destinations. By 1999, all but one of these companies had gone belly-up, and the lone survivor was operating in and out of bankruptcy. The bold reach for the benefits of competition was thwarted by the blunt realities of the marketplace.

During this shake-out period, David Neeleman was sitting on the sidelines cooling his passion for the airline business in the face of the grim realities of getting into the game. He gained a toehold by first creating a packaged tour business and later founding a small travel company. In short order, the business failed, clobbered by the roiling dynamics of a turbulent industry. After a short stint doing menial jobs at a family-owned grocery store, he hooked up with June Morris, owner of the largest travel agency in Utah. Together, they launched Morris Air as a charter operator to support the company's packaged tours. The tour business grew to the point that Morris morphed into a scheduled carrier, flying customers to several West Coast destinations. Rock-bottom prices coupled with high-quality service began to encroach on the turf of major airlines. A competitor complained to the Department of Transportation that Morris was flying regular routes with only charter status. The feds fined Morris but subsequently licensed the company to fly a regular schedule anywhere in the country. That gave Neeleman the incentive to strive to become a smaller version of Southwest, then the country's most successful airline.

At first, Morris operated as a Southwest knock-off, flying Boeing 737s to underserved airports and copying Southwest's quick turn-arounds, low fares, no-frills format, and fun-filled in-flight service.

But Neeleman added another wrinkle—electronic ticketing, so that a traveler could reserve directly with the airline, charge it to a credit card, show identification at the airport, and board the flight. No middleman. No ticket. At the time this was heresy, but it was another feature that propelled Morris to success. All this attracted the attention of competing airlines, most notably Southwest.

Southwest had previously expanded through growth rather than acquisition. But Morris's route structure and compatible culture were too attractive to pass up. In 1994, the deal was cut and Morris became part of Southwest. The union was celebrated in a lavish Las Vegas wedding ceremony coupling Morris magic with Southwest spirit. The merger was a success and Neeleman became a senior executive of Southwest. Problems arose when Neeleman pushed Southwest CEO Herb Kelleher to change to advance reservations and electronic ticketing. These ideas didn't fit at Southwest, and the airline wasn't big enough for two wizards in the executive suite, especially when the newcomer couldn't keep his mouth shut. In May, Herb took David to dinner and fired him, reportedly saying, "Everyone thinks you're a pain, even your biggest supporter."[101]

By now the airline business was in Neeleman's blood. His five-year noncompete agreement with Southwest provided an opportunity for some soul-searching. He identified his next quest—to create "the first mega-start-up in aviation history."[102] He envisioned an airline committed to restoring humanity in air travel, combining low fares with high style. His wizardry gave birth to an airline that is now one of the top-performing enterprises in the country—in terms of both profitability and customer satisfaction.

1. *Wizards are wise.*

From the get-go Neeleman realized he needed to surround himself with true believers whose talents complemented his strengths and compensated for his weaknesses. He plucked stars from other airlines to compose a dream team of people who would be attractive to investors as well as capable of launching a new venture. "His plan . . .

was not just to make a profit. It was to find like-minded individuals who wanted to shake up the airline establishment, who shared his vision for how to change the status quo."[103] He persuaded John Owen of Southwest to come aboard to manage the financial details. Ann Rhodes, also of Southwest, was selected to import the sense of a "warrior culture." From Continental Airlines, David Barger was recruited to watch over day-to-day operations. Barger became the yang to Neeleman's yin, grappling with the nuts and bolts of day-to-day management while Neeleman focused on magic and the big picture. Tom Kelly, an old friend, became general counsel to provide legal advice. On paper, the concept had the leadership talent to make a go of it.

2. *Wizards recognize the importance of symbols and emblematic events.*

Names are important. One of the first and most daunting tasks the new leadership encountered was to name their creation. Neeleman selected New Air as a temporary placeholder. No one thought that captured the essence of what they wanted to build, but what was the alternative? Finding a name became the vehicle for a deeper struggle about identity and meaning. Below the surface of almost endless deliberations was a search for the soul of the airline. The group considered many options, some more ludicrous than others: "Fair Air," "It," "Air Hop." Outside ad agencies were retained to help, charging fat rates for puny results. The group finally concluded that the name had to come from inside. The awesome responsibility was theirs. With a fleet of new Airbus A320 airplanes rolling from the assembly line, a decision had to be made. The only name the group could agree on was True Blue, but it felt like a weak compromise. Finally, seemingly from nowhere, the name JetBlue was hatched and the airline had the beginnings of an identity.

JetBlue was launched with a noble purpose—"bringing humanity back to air travel."[104] To fulfill this overarching mission, Neeleman and his associates identified a set of core values. Topping the list was passenger safety. The five others all focused on people—customers and employees. Concerned about mission statements that hang on walls rather than live in practice, they framed the values as leadership principles:

1. Treat your people right

2. Do the right thing

3. Communicate with your team

4. Encourage initiative and innovation

5. Inspire greatness in others[105]

When pilots, cabin attendants, and other employees are hired, JetBlue begins its indoctrination. New hires either "drink the blue Kool-Aid" or look for a job with a company more suited to their skills and temperament. A great deal of time is devoted to finding and hiring the "right people." Intense initiation rites weed out those who don't align with the cultural norms and values.

But culture, "the way we do things around here," needs constant reinforcement. JetBlue provides this symbolic support to customers in the form of comforts such as leather seats, each with its own private TV. More important, culture is communicated through ritual, ceremonies, and stories. Barger and Neeleman convene annual "speak-up" events to give employees a voice in airing their views and to provide an opportunity for top executives to sketch the big picture. Headquarters end-of-week picnics provide a welcome relief from day-to-day trials and tribulations and a chance to connect with others in a fun environment. Neeleman credits these occasions as a prime factor in the airline's success, the nontangible "Kumbayah stuff" that knits the company together and creates the magic that rivets everyone on the nitty-gritty that assures customer satisfaction.[106]

Even in its infancy, JetBlue accumulated a treasure trove of stories. Most celebrate the company's beyond-the-call-of-duty efforts to accommodate customers, buttressing JetBlue's higher calling, "restoring humanity to air travel." On 9/11, all U.S. flights were grounded and passengers were stranded across the country. At New York's Kennedy airport, JetBlue took care of its passengers—and other airlines' customers as well. When told to evacuate its terminal, JetBlue announced that "all present, no matter whose customers they were, could go with them to a nearby airport hotel, where they could stay until they had someplace else to go."[107] Neeleman had already authorized everyone in the field to do what their conscience suggested, regardless of the expense. When the airport reopened, passengers returned—much to the chagrin of other airlines—sporting JetBlue T-shirts. Passengers marooned in Europe were—free of charge— ferried back to the United States on a new Airbus 320 that was being delivered to JetBlue.[108]

On another occasion, a customer learned that his mother was dying. He called Delta Airlines to check on a bereavement fare. He was quoted the normal ticket price of $800. When he pushed further about a special fare given the circumstances, the agent said, "That depends, has she died yet?" The man then checked JetBlue and was immediately quoted the lowest fare possible. He became a regular customer.[109]

3. *Wizards encourage a strong link between words and deeds.*

Nothing drives a wedge between people's aspirations and accomplishments more quickly than hypocrisy. Neeleman and his associates consistently practice what they preach. Neeleman, for example, is a regular feature on flights, serving beverages and snacks along with the cabin crews. He has acquired an apron embroidered with the title "Snack Boy." This paid off with Norm Brodsky, a writer for *Inc.* magazine, on a flight from New York to California. Brodsky was surprised to see Neeleman making an announcement at the front of the cabin. "Hi," he said, "my name is Dave Neeleman, and I'm the CEO of JetBlue. I'm here to serve you this evening, and I'm looking forward to meeting each of you before we land."[110] Brodsky was more surprised to find that Neeleman spent time with every passenger. But he was bowled over when, half an hour after they had chatted, Neeleman returned to tell him, "One of your *Inc.* colleagues is on the plane. She says you don't know her, but she'd like to meet you."[111] Already a JetBlue fan, Brodsky offered *Inc.*'s frequent-flyer readers a glowing review of JetBlue, saying he was inspired to redouble his efforts to get more CEOs to learn from Neeleman's example.

The success of JetBlue owes much to the wizardry of David Neeleman. His magic has put the airline on a trajectory to set an example of how to create something special in an industry notorious for making travel an odious experience.

WIZARDRY IN THE CULINARY ARTS

Yountville, in the heart of California's Napa Valley, has a population of about three thousand in a land area less than two square miles. Despite its size, the town is blessed with one of the finest restaurants in the world—the French Laundry. It can take years to get a reservation. Would-be patrons sometimes skip the phone call and travel to the restaurant in hopes that a personal plea can cut the waiting period to six months. Dining at the French Laundry goes well beyond eating great food. It is a magical experience. The head chef, Thomas Keller, is a culinary wizard who transforms ordinary ingredients into unforgettable, edible works of art. His patrons depart with a mystical appreciation of what a talented wizard can accomplish. Deepak Chopra's characterization of a wizard fits Keller to a T: "A wizard can turn the time bound into the timeless. A wizard can take you beyond limitations into the boundless."[112]

Keller wasn't born a wizard, nor was he formally trained in the culinary arts. Many chefs stake their reputations on a prestigious certificate from the Culinary Institute of America. During their residency at the Institute, aspiring chefs learn to master the standards and techniques of creating haute cuisine. They learn perfection in duplicating famous dishes passed through generations of top French chefs. But as Michael Ruhlman points out, the Institute teaches the basic skills and techniques. It doesn't teach soul.[113]

Keller took a different route—a journey through all aspects of the restaurant business, absorbing everything he could along the way. He began on the bottom rung of the restaurant functional chain as a dishwasher, and learned by figuring out things for himself.

1. *Wizards plunge wholeheartedly into unfamiliar depths.*

Keller did not set out with the goal of becoming a top chef, but each step he took nudged him in that direction. As Chopra points out in his lessons on becoming a wizard, "Every desire is created by some past desire. The chain of desires never ends. It is life itself."[114] Keller immersed himself in a series of challenges and let the flow take him wherever it led. After stints dealing with everything from prep to dishwashing drudgery in support of other chefs' creations, Keller became a chef at the Palm Beach Yacht Club. The step up was not that dramatic, mainly flipping hamburgers while pursuing an emerging dream of more refined cooking. He moved on to become a line cook at various eateries in Florida and parts north. A chance beach encounter with Roland Henin, one of New England's top chefs, created new opportunities, first on the cook line under Henin's watchful tutorial eye and then as his saucier and student:

> Henin taught me that cooking was not just a job. . . . He took me aside; he showed me the reasons *he* cooked. It was about being creative, gratification, satisfying yourself and satisfying people; that that was the raison d'être to feed people and ultimately to feed yourself. As you're feeding others, you're feeding yourself; you're getting the fuel to push yourself forward. He taught me about passion.[115]

That valuable lesson pushed Keller into several more jobs, cooking on his own and working for others. It was later to become the foundation for the French Laundry, and Keller was destined to realize his quest, to become "a Buddhist monk in search of perfection."[116]

2. *Wizards are passionate.*

Keller poured his heart and soul into his dream. Losses piled up in the French Laundry's early months, but he staunchly refused to compromise his high standards: "I was in the shit, but I kept my focus on the food."[117] That commitment ran deep: "You have to have an enormous respect for food. . . . It's why I killed the rabbits."[118] Originally rabbits came to him already dressed. He decided to butcher them himself, as a reminder that all food has a source in real life. Each rabbit's sacrifice meant something and deserved to be honored, not wasted. Even a lowly turnip, or a set of duck testicles or pork ears, was treated with reverence. Fresh fish were put on ice in the same position they swam to avoid stressing their flesh—"cradled as carefully as a newborn child." All raw ingredients played a part of Keller's desire to feed other people and "make them swoon."

3. *Wizards are transformers, turning the status quo into something special.*

A good chef distills the essence of simple things into something distinctive. Keller "reduced the extraordinary range of food at his disposal and distilled it or brought it through careful cooking to the state in which its fundamental and enduring essences are available where they were not before—whether with a carrot, a truffle, duck tongue, or beef short rib."[119] Keller prided himself on taking second or third cuts and elevating them to a level of culinary distinction. Cooking, like leadership, is a series of skillful manipulations aimed at achieving something of shared value or worth from what is at hand. Ever the wizard, combining Zen-like spirituality with a sense of groundedness, Keller has been able to achieve a noble purpose: cooking for people and making them happy.

4. *Wizards tie a familiar past with a new reality.*

Leaders often attempt to impose a new order on the status quo. People have trouble adjusting to innovative ideas and practices because attachments to traditional ways are severed. Keller avoided this trap by putting a new twist on familiar and comfortable food. His oyster and pearls creation combines caviar and oysters with tapioca pudding, "perfuming, with worldly elegance and luxurious seduction, remembered comforts of childhood, enhancing the bland pudding with . . . ocean salt."[120] His grilled cheese sandwich builds on memories of Wonder bread and American cheese, but transforms them into slices of brioche and farmhouse cheddar, grilled and served with clear tomato water and thin potato chips fried in clarified butter and sprinkled with caraway powder. In Keller's words: "There you have it, a composed plate that resembles something you grew up with, but still it's creative haute cuisine."[121] Keller's spin on an all-too-familiar comfort food retains its "mac and cheese" title. But at the French Laundry it is magically recast as butter-poached lobster on creamy orzo topped with a Parmesan crisp. The creative combination of familiar and novel moves diners up a notch on the food appreciation scale without threatening their comfort zone.

AUTHENTIC WIZARDRY AND EXCELLENCE

Both Neeleman and Keller have created organizations that excel in their respective industries. They have succeeded where many others have failed by adhering to some enduring principles:

- Searching deeply within their souls for answers to basic life questions: Who am I? What do I value and hold most dear? And what contribution will I make to the world of work?

- Being willing to take short-term risks to achieve long-term passions and aspirations.

- Drawing others into the fold by creating symbols that really matter.

- Reinforcing shared values through their own behavior and continual vigilance to maintain the faith.

- Cherishing dreams while confronting head-on the realities of a complex and turbulent world that nibbles away at ideals.

Prevailing wisdom and evidence point to a shared core of values and beliefs, uniting people in a common quest, as a prime ingredient in organizational success. But too many leaders shirk their wizardly responsibilities by neglecting magic and instead devoting most of their time to immediate and tangible tasks. Even if they solve every problem that comes their way, their people and their organizations lose any sense of magic and mission. Where will the wizards emerge that will create or transform organizations to equal the enchanting spiritual examples of JetBlue and the French Laundry? A source of answers is close at hand. As Chopra observes, "A wizard exists in all of us. This wizard sees and knows everything and nature reflects the mood of this wizard."[122] Leaders need to find and express their own magic.

11

THE WANNABE WIZARD

Wannabe wizards are never in short supply. They are often graduates of elite leadership training programs. They have been steeped in the most fashionable theories about what makes organizations tick and the latest strategies for making them work better. They are pumped up at the prospect of single-handedly wresting major improvements and sizable profits from a sluggish status quo. They have few doubts that they can pull off a miraculous new venture or turnaround. Then they plan to move on to bigger and better challenges.

*W*annabe wizards veer off the road when their bold new ideas go nose-to-nose with traditional values and entrenched cultural ways. What looked like an open road turns out to be a minefield. Wannabes also go astray when they initiate a bold new undertaking with vacuous values and cotton candy platitudes that offer little meaning or substance. The resulting vacuum attracts time-worn ways imported from other circumstances and creates a breeding ground for greed and destructive politics. Unlike streetwise authentic wizards, wannabes rely too heavily on book smarts and the fashionable ideas of the moment. They become caught up in their noble intentions and anticipated success, only to trip over unforeseen events. Their intended magic proves no match for the power of opposing forces.

KEN LAY: ENRON'S WANNABE WIZARD

In the autumn of 2001, the Enron Corporation, a high-flying business success, crumbled. The company's precipitous fall from grace resembles the fabled fate of Icarus, whose father Daedalus produced a set of waxen wings so the young man could fly. The gift came with a stern warning: "Don't fly too high or the heat of the sun will melt your wings." Icarus was soon seduced by the thrill of flying. Forgetting that his wings were vulnerable, he flew too close to the sun and, wingless, dropped to his death.

Kenneth Lay had grown up dirt poor in rural Missouri, but he was determined not to stay that way. Trained as an economist, he was eager to make his mark and make some money in the business world. After stints in the Navy and at Exxon, he worked in Washington in the early days of energy deregulation and rose to a position as deputy undersecretary of energy. Then he took a job with a gas pipeline business in Florida and rose quickly. He moved to Houston and eventually found himself CEO of a newly merged pipeline company that gave itself a new name—Enron.

Lay was ahead of the curve in seeing the financial and entrepreneurial possibilities of energy deregulation, and of changing the heavily regulated pipeline industry into a spot market financial player. His early success made him a legendary figure in the industry and greased the skids for the birth of an enterprise that quickly became the darling of Wall Street and the pride of Houston. Under Lay's leadership, Enron's revenues grew from $10 billion in 1985 to $100 billion in 2000. During the same period, Enron's market value shot up nearly fifty-fold, from $2 billion to almost $96 billion. It was Lay's company and he believed deeply in its robust future. His confidence was shared by others inside the company as well as by well-placed business and political leaders, including the president of the United States, George W. Bush. Ken Lay was widely portrayed as a magician who had produced one of the great miracles in modern business. No one, including Ken Lay, could fully grasp or articulate the secrets of Enron's success. It seemed almost mystical.

When the ethereal bubble burst, its impact was felt across the board. Employees lost their jobs and homes, as did many unwary investors. Houston was thrown into economic chaos. But the ruinous effects cut an even wider swath:

> Arthur Andersen, the once-revered accounting firm, evaporated overnight as its role in the debacle led to a subsidiary scandal of its own. A president and members of his administration, already struggling with a new threat to national security, found themselves on the defensive because of their close association with Enron. The new chairman of the Securities and Exchange Commission saw his dream job slip through his fingers amid the recriminations. And members of Congress, reacting to their constituents' fear and anger, pushed through what proved to be the most dramatic revision since the Great Depression in the laws protecting investors.[123]

Blame for this widespread tragedy had to come home to roost somewhere. One of the obvious targets was Ken Lay, whose image shifted almost overnight from acclaimed corporate genius to despised villain. But a closer, more detached look reveals an executive guilty more of misfeasance than malfeasance. Ken Lay was a genial man of deep faith who regularly gave pep talks about Enron's high ethical standards. He was also a hands-off manager who had trouble making decisions that might anger anyone and preferred staying above the fray as the company's Mr. Outside.[124] Lay recalled occasions when he had weighed in against questionable deals. In Enron's tailspin, he found it hard to grasp why outsiders were howling mad about Enron's accounting practices: "We had every protection in place. We disclosed it all. They just don't understand."[125] As the company imploded Lay cashed in stock options and rallied employees to hold on to theirs. Was that lying? Or was it the result of normal cash-out process and a heartfelt faith and belief that Enron would right itself and continue its pattern of phenomenal growth and profitability? As Lay told Mike Wallace in a *Sixty Minutes* interview: "I'm not a fool, I was fooled." Rather than being a villainous schemer and liar, Ken Lay played a role in the Enron debacle that exemplifies some of a wannabe wizard's blind spots and frailties:

1. ***Underestimating the influence of the environment on organizational values and practices.***

Particularly in new companies, values and beliefs from outside impact internal workings. Newness has not given local ways an opportunity to emerge and mature. Consequently what the CEO wants and expects may run counter to what actually happens. When the late Marvin Runyan, CEO of Nissan of America, became CEO of a new car company he was handed a blank slate, Very soon, however, he realized the behavior of employees was shaped more by where they had come from (Ford, Chevrolet, or Chrysler) than the direction he wanted them to head.

In Enron's case, the environment penetrated every corner of the new organization. During that period, the business world was casting off regulation in favor of unbridled competition. Without any internal filters, Enron quickly became a mirror of the times:

> Across corporate America, widespread corner cutting, steadily falling standards, and compromised financial discipline had been festering for close to a decade. Warnings about funny numbers, unrealistic expectations and the coming pain of economic reality went unheeded as investors happily bought into the promises of corporations pursuing reckless or incomprehensible business strategies, enabling their stock prices to defy the laws of gravity.[126]

In a sense, Ken Lay was never fully in control of Enron. External forces ran the show and determined the corporation's destiny.

2. *Discounting the significance of symbols and cultural values and practices.*

Flags and anthems hold nations together. Colors signify a gang's identity and bond members to each other in blood pacts. Recent studies of top-performing businesses have, time and again, highlighted cultural cohesion and focus as a key factor in financial performance.[127] But Enron paid little attention to what the company stood for and held most dear. Profits and stock price were almost the exclusive cultural focal point. For lack of attention, even potentially rich symbolic occasions were feeble and fumbling. Enron's logo, the tilted E, was introduced to executives and employees in a lavish, dramatic corporate ceremony. Lay's introduction predicted a robust future for the logo and the company it would represent: "It will be recognized as the logo of a company leading the energy industry into the next century, into the next millennium."[128] Those in attendance were impressed and even more excited when they returned to work to find the tilted E displayed everywhere.

But everything went downhill from there. As the logo was faxed worldwide, the yellow middle prong of the E disappeared, yielding a facsimile of an electric plug. Worse yet, to Italian eyes it looked like an obscene gesture. Failure to attend to important details rendered the logo useless and cost the company millions of dollars in its creation and subsequent modification. An important corporate symbol became a well-known cultural screwup.

3. *Overlooking the importance of corporate heroes and heroines.*

In distributing recognition and rewards, Lay and his leadership team missed another opportunity to define the company's values. They reinforced only what mattered most: profit whatever its source. One of the most visible representations of cultural values is an anointed pantheon of corporate heroes. Heroes and heroines are living icons serving as signs and signals of what a company stands for and values. At Enron it was clear—whoever bagged the latest lucrative deal was singled out for lavish praise and a hefty paycheck. Other important cultural players were ignored, overlooked, and underpaid. One example was Jim Bouillon, the executive in charge of purchasing business insurance. In Enron's heyday, he was seen as irrelevant beside the deal makers. Executives joked that a monkey could handle his job. His salary year after year reflected the disdain he was accorded, until the company's collapse suddenly made his work vital:

> The executive whose contribution had been waved aside by top officers as insignificant, not in the same league as the work done by the whiz kids who put together deals like the Raptors, [was now a champion]. . . . The financial structures and machinations so celebrated by [top executives] were all gone; only Jim Bouillon's insurance remained. And now the executives who had once dismissed him as a nobody clung to his top-notch work like a life raft, hoping it would protect them from the hundreds of lawsuits they now faced.[129]

Ironically, it was Sherron Watkins, one of Enron's unsung heroines, who became the whistle-blower who brought the company down.

4. *Getting caught up in your own image and neglecting the business.*

Without a doubt, Enron was Ken Lay and Ken Lay was Enron. Lay spent much of his time hobnobbing with high government officials and celebrities. He was on a first-name basis with President Bush and members of his cabinet. He golfed with legends of the game. He attended lavish parties and hosted many of his own. He trusted others to manage the business, trust that was too often misplaced. In this vacuum, wheeler-dealers concocted off-the-books deals and pushed legal boundaries with little oversight. It was like a gold rush in a town with no sheriff. As long as profits and the stock price went up, Lay felt comfortable in his high-rolling world and continued to give his subordinates free rein. Many of the deal makers were young products of elite grad schools who were technically sophisticated but deficient in experience and judgment. Many became wealthy at the company's expense. Chief deal maker Andy Fastow pulled millions of dollars out of off-the-books partnerships for himself and his family and friends. Even at the end, Lay had no inkling that Fastow had been running rampant with highly questionable deals. As whistle-blower Sherron Watkins tried to explain how Fastow's deals could bring down the company, Lay asked plaintively, "Andy's a good CFO, right? He's doing a good job, right?"[130]

Ken Lay was a wannabe wizard. He wanted to create the greatest company ever to grace the world of business. At first the magic seemed to work, but a cultural vacuum allowed greed and cutthroat politics to trample the high ethical standards he espoused. Lay wanted an innovative, profitable, and harmonious company. He wound up with a seething cauldron of selfish individuals seeking wealth without meaning:

> Enron's fate was not simply the outgrowth of rampant lawbreaking. The true story was more complex, and certainly more disturbing. For

crime at Enron—and, no doubt, there was crime—was just one ingredient of the toxic stew that poisoned the company. Shocking incompetence, unjustified arrogance, compromised ethics, and an utter contempt for the market's judgment all played decisive roles. Ultimately, it was Enron's tragedy to be filled with people smart enough to know how to maneuver around the rules—but not wise enough to understand why the rules had been written in the first place.[131]

CARLY FIORINA: HP'S FALLEN STAR

Until the late 1990s, Hewlett-Packard (HP) was one of the most admired companies both in the United States and abroad. It had a mystical ring, a spirit that captured the hearts and souls of people inside and outside the corporation. "Put simply, it seemed HP had figured out the magical formula for how to run a company. Everyone won—investors, customers, managers, and employees."[132] The company's financial success hinged on the "HP way," which articulated and embraced revered cultural values: humility, respect for the individual, hard work, frugality, teamwork, and integrity. These values shaped behavior across the board. Adherence was rewarded; deviance was chastised.

The Hewlett-Packard cultural code was the brainchild of the company's founders—Bill Hewlett and David Packard. The two engineers began their careers tinkering in a Palo Alto garage. Before long, their puttering paid off in innovative new products and HP was on its way to becoming a Silicon Valley legend. As the company grew, stories of Bill and Dave, coupled with rituals, ceremonies, and other cultural customs and traditions, knit the enterprise together as a meaningful, unified, and focused business. In the truest sense of the term, Bill and Dave were wizards who worked magic in creating an enterprise that worked—until the late 1980s.

HP's troubles began to appear when the company tried to compete in the emerging and stormy personal computer industry. HP thrived on new products, but struggled to be a viable contender in personal computers. Its only great success was in printers, which soon became the company's primary source of profits.

In the meantime, the HP way was starting to unravel. Some people still clung to the traditional values and practices as gospel: others ridiculed the principles and used them to justify multiple parochial agendas and approaches. By the latter part of the 1980s, HP was no longer a unified and focused enterprise. Three subcultures competed with one another for attention and resources: the traditional electronic instrument business, the remnants of the computer initiatives, and the thriving printer venture. Politics and bureaucracy dominated day-to-day operations. Company spirit sagged. HP was losing its soul. Hewlett and Packard were no longer there to restore the magic. And the leadership the company did have was not up to the challenge.

In 1997 HP started missing its financial targets. This downslide continued into early 1999 when the board stepped in. HP had lost its aggressiveness and confidence. Managing the company was in one executive's opinion a day-to-day exercise in "herding cats." The board of directors saw a need for drastic action and new leadership to shake things up: "HP needed a leader who could change the culture without breaking it, someone with a gentle touch and a spine of steel."[133] The search eventually settled on Carly Fiorina, a trophy CEO with the background and potential to wave a wand and restore the magic.

Fiorina was bright, extremely articulate, and very charismatic. In most ways, she was everything HP wasn't, and initially she was smart enough to play that card right. She struck a deal with Dick Hackborn, head of HP's highly successful printing division, to make him chairman of the board during her initial time as CEO. Her proposal: that he represented "so much of what is the true soul and spirit of HP" that the two of them could become a powerful odd couple representing a balance between tradition and innovation.[134] Fiorina had been briefed about the power of the HP culture. Many board members saw the need for drastic change, and one had told a CEO candidate, "The first thing we have to do is get rid of the HP Way."[135] But most employees were still attached to tradition. Fiorina was forewarned about the consequences of going head-to-head with entrenched cultural values and customs: "They are going to come after you, and you'd better be ready. And because you are a woman, the antibodies may come after you harder than they would otherwise."[136]

Fiorina's short reign at HP suggested she never really got the message. Like other wannabe wizards hired to turn a company around, she relied too heavily on her vision and charisma but had little sense of opposing cultural forces that generated resistance and counterattacks.

1. *Promoting self rather than shining the spotlight on the company's past and future.*

Fiorina's selection was obviously newsworthy—the first woman to lead a Fortune 50 corporation. She was a natural performer who took advantage of every media opportunity pitched her way. Unlike Lou Gerstner, who quietly entered a similar situation at IBM, Fiorina grabbed the spotlight, eclipsing the efforts of thousands of people whose day-to-day efforts could make or break the company's performance. In a short time, many employees began to suspect her motives. Their doubts were exacerbated by the fact that her personal fanfare violated a core HP value—humility.

2. *Overpromising and raising unrealistic expectations.*

In November 1999 Fiorina made a promise she couldn't keep—that HP would grow 12 to 15 percent annually. At IBM, Lou Gerstner did the opposite: underpromised and overdelivered. In raising expectations early on, Fiorina gained the short-term support of the board and shareholders, but paid the piper later when the company missed its targets. Unrealistic optimism may produce immediate gratification, but it saddles a leader with debt plus interest in the future.

3. *Surrounding oneself with like-minded loyalists.*

Wannabe wizards dislike criticism and bad news. Fiorina insulated herself with a group of mostly younger acolytes with little operational experience. These true believers came to be known as "Carly's Cult," slavishly devoted to Fiorina and her agenda for changing HP. As one member of the cult put it, "I don't just stir the Kool-Aid. I drink it."[137] This tight group of loyalists created a barrier insulating Fiorina from HP veterans and naysayers who knew what was going on in hallways, bathrooms, and after-hours meeting places. As a result, Fiorina rarely got information she needed about what was really happening in the company.

4. *Riding roughshod over sacred cultural totems and taboos.*

Cultural totems and taboos provide symbolic signposts for what to do and what to avoid as a member of a social or work group. Most are unwritten. Some are obvious if you are privy to the cultural code. Others are subtle. As wannabe wizards try to create new organizations or transform existing ones, they too often shirk or overlook their symbolic duties. Fiorina never seemed to fully understand the power the HP culture still retained, even though it had become diluted or tattered over time. Consequently, she made classic blunders that accumulated to undercut her moral authority:

- Publishing a new "Rules of the Garage," an updated version of Hewlett and Packard's original objectives, which employees perceived as trite marketing musings.

- Flying first class when everyone else traveled coach. Later adding two new Gulfstream jets to HP's aging fleet of planes and restricting their use to top executives.

- Having an ad agency superimpose her image, standing next to Hewlett and Packard in front of the legendary garage, birthplace of the company.

- Driving a sporty convertible rather than the HP standard-issue Ford Taurus.

- Hiring a personal bodyguard and beefing up security for other top executives.

- Giving speeches too polished and sophisticated to appear authentic. As one employee put it, "She's an eloquent idiot. She speaks very well, but she doesn't know what she's talking about."[138]

- Hiring a helicopter in Paris to take her to several meetings and felling trees around HP's Paris headquarters to provide access for take-off and landing.

- Keeping a very low profile around HP's Silicon Valley offices when her predecessors had been visible and approachable.

- Replacing Dockers with Armani suits as the encouraged dress code.

- Firing people without looking them in the eye and letting them know why they were being let go.

- Gravely underestimating the symbolic power of a family name in her emotionally charged public battle with Walter Hewlett over the Compaq merger.

None of these actions was egregious by itself. But woven together in the context of HP's distinctive culture, they foretold a disappointing conclusion to Carly Fiorina's reign.

Unlike authentic wizards, whose magic breathes spirit and soul into an enterprise, wannabe wizards have great intentions but limited ability to create a meaningful organization or transform one in trouble. They lack the symbolic intelligence and sensitivity to make it happen. Unfortunately, many contemporary organizations have one of these wannabes at the helm right now.

12

THE HARMFUL WIZARD

Authentic wizards apply their wisdom and magic to create or transform successful organizations. Wannabe wizards pursue worthy goals and have the potential to make good things happen, but through inaction, error, or mental darkness never quite pull it off. Their intentions are noble, but their execution is flawed.

armful wizards are another breed. The Wicked Witch of the East in *Wizard of Oz*. Lord Voldemort in the Harry Potter series. Sauron in *The Lord of the Rings*. Their objectives are self-serving, sinister—or both. They leverage their magic with a profound understanding of the potency of symbols, but manipulate people toward questionable ends. The end justifies the means. In the short term they are often successful. But in the end their schemes lead to chaos and destruction. Others pay the price for their grandiose, fanatical, or destructive visions.

History abounds with the misguided exploits of harmful wizards. Napoleon Bonaparte, Adolph Hitler, Joseph Stalin, Pol Pot, Slobodan Milosevic, Saddam Hussein, and Osama bin Laden, to name a few. America's corporate world has also seen its share of talented executives whose evil feats of magic wreak havoc on others: Eastern Airline's Frank Lorenzo, Sunbeam's "Chainsaw" Al Dunlap, WorldCom's Bernie Ebbers. The magic is potent; the aftermath is calamitous.

ANDREW FASTOW: ENRON'S PRINCE OF DARKNESS

Andrew Fastow was a wizard of deal making—esoteric transactions, voodoo financing, derivatives, and leveraged buy-outs. It started when he was a boy; one of his high school teachers remembered him as a wheeler-dealer who negotiated for higher grades.[139] After college, he took a job with Continental Bank in Chicago, where he wound up working with a group that was pioneering "securitization"—an eso-teric financial art that involves finding creative ways to put old finan-cial assets into attractive new bottles that fetch a higher price. Fastow was viewed by his associates as able but nakedly ambitious and too willing to push the legal limits on deals. As one colleague said, "I don't know that he ever had a moral compass."[140] At Continental, Fastow had training wheels to keep him out of trouble, because his bosses rejected his flakier proposals.

But then he went to Enron. Enron's chief operating officer, Jeffrey Skilling, was looking for a securitization maven who could transform some of Enron's sow's ears into silk purses, thus freeing up capital to reinvest in the business. Skilling was impressed by Fastow's glittering résumé. He didn't know that much of it was exaggerated, and the two hit it off in Fastow's job interview. Once at Enron, Fastow was given a green light to pump up the bottom line of a traditional pipeline company. There was little guidance about how—Enron prided itself on innovation and on giving talented and ambitious people room to do great things. With the blessing of CEO Kenneth Lay and second-in-command Skilling, Fastow enjoyed minimal oversight.

Fastow started at Enron in 1990, and he rose rapidly on the strength of his deal-making skills. He soon became known for his ambition and overt sucking up to Skilling. It was less obvious that Fastow had little business and financial know-how outside deal making. In one meeting with outside analysts, Fastow was asked how he managed the interest rate exposure in his various deals. When he responded, "I don't have any," his audience was aghast. After Fastow left the meeting, one analyst remarked: "That guy has already lost the company a few million dollars, and he doesn't even know it yet."[141]

Fastow's limitations were revealed again when Skilling asked him to head up a new retail gas business and produce a business plan. After several feeble efforts, he gave up and asked Skilling to let him go back to doing deals. When Enron needed a new chief financial officer, Lay and Skilling originally planned to hire an outsider. But Fastow and Rick Causey, Enron's accounting chief, teamed up to say neither one would work for the leading candidate. Lay and Skilling backed off and gave the CFO job to Fastow. He was in far over his head. He knew so little about accounting that some colleagues doubted he could really read a balance sheet. The CFO is responsible for ensuring the company's financial strength, but "Andy didn't have a risk-control bone in his body."[142] It was akin to asking the fox to guard the chicken coop. Fastow had no background in finance and the department soon became a profit center, with everyone jockeying to close the next big deal. The sheriff who was supposed to say no to over-the-top deals was Fastow's buddy, Rick Causey. The two developed a partnership. Causey's accountants would alert Fastow whenever there was a potential shortfall in Enron's profit forecasts—and then help ensure that the right deals closed at the right time to solve the problem.

As time went on and Enron had increasing difficulty finding profit growth, the deals became bigger and more audacious. One that Fastow and one of his loyal minions, Michael Kopper (head of special projects), cobbled together was a structured transaction that required outside investors to provide 3 percent of the deal's capital. Under the rules, a company could provide 97 percent of the capital to an off-books "special purpose entity" (SPE), find 3 percent somewhere else, stir in some legal legerdemain, and—poof!—an "independent" buyer was created. Enron could then legally "sell" assets to the SPE—even if most of the payment came from its own pockets. The round trip of cash complete, the company had converted an asset into revenue. When Andersen accountants first laid out the rules, Fastow had ridiculed them, saying the 3 percent could come from anybody—even his gardener or his family. Now he was ready to back up his words.

With Kopper's help, he constructed an entity called Alpine Investors to make the purchase. It would cost about $17 million, far more than Fastow had in his bank account. But with the magic of structured finance, he didn't have to worry about that. Almost $16.5 million would come in a loan to Alpine from Enron. Then Fastow—along with his wife's wealthy family, the Weingartens, and friends like Patty Melcher, a wealthy Houstonian close to Fastow's wife, Lea—would kick in $510,000. Fastow would run the partnership, with Enron's friends as investors.[143]

When this plan failed to pass the scrutiny of accountants because of the family involvement, Fastow reached more deeply into his magic bag of tricks:

> He sought out Kopper, and together they devised a solution—a dishonest one. They needed $510,000 but had raised only $91,000 from wealthy Houstonians they knew. The rest, $419,000, would be put up by Fastow but made to look as though it came from someone else. The cash went to Kopper from the Fastows' account, with Lea writing records showing it as a loan. Kopper then funneled the

money to his domestic partner, Bill Dodson, and to Kathy Wetmore, the Fastows' real estate agent. Both agreed to act as fronts for Fastow, pretending the money was theirs. With a little money laundering, Fastow had pulled off the very deal that the accountants had said couldn't be done—at least not legally.[144]

This tangled web of manipulation and deception set the pattern for subsequent transactions, now formally housed as a special projects SWAT team within the finance division. So-called independent partnerships multiplied, all guaranteed by Enron. The transactions invariably prettied up Enron's bottom line. But Fastow and his cronies reaped the lion's share of the profits—without any of the risks.

To head off internal questioning or interference, Fastow drew several key executives into his schemes, including his protégé, Ben Glisan, an accountant in a position to review many of his deals, and Kristina Mordaunt, an in-house lawyer. For a short-term investment of $5,800 on one deal, these executives both walked away with over a million dollars in return. Those he could not co-opt, Fastow put off when they raised questions about his off-the-books dealings. Treasurer Jeff McMahon confronted Fastow about his communication with Enron's Tier 1 banks:

"I understand you've been calling on Enron's Tier 1 banks to invest in your new deal."

"Yeah, they're on our list."

"Well, that's a surprise to me, Andy. So I'm going to need to know what you're doing for this LJM2, who you're calling on, and who your investors are going to be."

Fastow squinched his face. "Why do you need to know *that?*" He asked sharply.

"Because I'm responsible for Enron's banking relationships."

"This has nothing to do with Enron," Fastow snapped.

"Well, these banks are calling up, saying they believe the deal you're pitching is, if you don't pay LJM2, they don't get to play at the Enron level."

Fastow snorted. "Oh, that's just not true."

"That's what their perception is."

"Well, they're wrong."

"Look, Andy," McMahon said. "We're dealing with perceptions, and I'm going to have to manage those. So I need a list of who you're calling, and who's making a commitment. That way, when they call me, I'll be prepared. And I can tell them that there's no connection between their decisions on LJM2 and their future Enron business."

Fastow thought about it for a second. "Yeah, you're right," he said. "I'll get you the list."[145]

Weeks passed and McMahon never received the list. He ran into Fastow in the hallway and reminded him about his past-due promise. Fastow seemed surprised and renewed his pledge. A week later, McMahon pulled Fastow aside after a meeting, and again asked him for the information he needed. Fastow gave him a sheepish look and said, "Oh yeah, you're right. I'll get right on it."[146] McMahon realized then that Fastow was lying and the list would never come. That was another of his ploys to hide his unscrupulous tricks. His "I'll fix it, trust me" guarantees were never genuine. For months, he vowed to move the special projects division's operations off the finance floor. This was a ruse to buy time. It never happened. Fastow's investment group was given free space and support as long as their off-the-books deals bolstered Enron's bottom line.

Fastow used his position at Enron to bully or buy off his opposition inside or outside the company. He promised a First Union banker the next Enron bond issue if he would invest in one of his special projects transactions. He made the same promises to others.

But when the time came, he reneged. All bets off. Threats to Fastow's operation were countered with ominous intimidation in the name of Enron. As treasurer McMahon admitted:

> "Andy knows he's got everybody by the balls," he said. "[Rick Buy, the Chief Risk Officer] just rubber-stamps those deals, and Andy rolls right over him. Andy's trying to get our bankers to invest with him and holding out a threat that they might lose Enron business if they don't. And Causey's [Chief Accounting Officer] in a big dilemma because, at the end of the day, he's responsible for the financial statements and LJM helps make the numbers."[147]

Fastow's shenanigans worked for several reasons. Lay and Skilling trusted him and were willing to sign off on everything as long as other relevant people signed off. They didn't realize the others were too enmeshed in the bogus transactions. More important, all Fastow's deals were based on the assumption that no questions would be asked and Enron's stock price would continue to rise.

Then a few skeptical analysts began to ask questions. The beginning of the end was Bethany McLean's cover story in the March 2001 issue of *Fortune,* under the title, "Is Enron Overpriced?" McLean wrote that Enron's financial statements were almost impenetrable, and it was very hard to get a clear answer to the simple question, "How does Enron make its money?" Soon thereafter, the *Wall Street Journal* and the U.S. government began to investigate, and the stock price began its precipitous fall. Fastow's wizardry collapsed once Enron's stock price could no longer keep his many partnerships solvent. One by one the transactions were exposed and the real beneficiary became obvious. With that, one of America's most successful and visible companies crumbled, making criminals of its executives and victims of its employees, investors, and countless others.

JIM JONES AND THE PEOPLE'S TEMPLE

The phrase "drinking the Kool-Aid" has entered the American lexicon, and at companies like Hewlett-Packard and JetBlue it is used as a way to talk about employees' signing up psychologically to embrace a company's mission and culture. It is a metaphoric borrowing based on the tragic story of Jim Jones and the People's Temple. At the temple, in a ritual that had been rehearsed before, people drank a grape-flavored concoction laced with cyanide and paid the ultimate price of loyalty.[148] More than nine hundred people sacrificed their lives to the cause. It is a grim testimony to the power of a wizard's magic in the form of omens, parables, liturgy, and potions.

Jim Jones attracted a following different from what you might expect for the son of a Ku Klux Klan member. Ordained as a Christian minister, Jones set his magic to work on the mission of creating an interracial mission for the sick, homeless, and jobless. He "preached a social gospel of human freedom, equality, and love." He emphasized helping the lowest of society's members and was not at all bashful in proclaiming his powers to produce miracles: "With over 4,000 members of our California church, we haven't had a death yet! . . . I am a prophet of God and I can cure both the illness of your body as well as illness of your mind."[149]

As his interracial group migrated from Indiana to Ukiah, California, and then to San Francisco, Jones attracted heavy skepticism and criticism from outsiders. But the People's Temple was still able to garner support from other faith-based programs and kind words in the media. The *Washington Post's* Katherine Graham wrote: "Please extend my thanks to Jim Jones for his interest in such issues as the free press and free speech."[150] Investigative reporter Jack Anderson commented: "It's a wonderful thing that your Church and Rev. Jones are doing." Even *San Francisco Chronicle* curmudgeon Herb Caen counted Jim Jones as a friend—"although he couldn't show it too openly."[151]

Below the surface, Jim Jones was unraveling emotionally and spiritually. More and more, he relied on coercive force rather than wizardly magic to hold his group together. Rumors began to circulate outside the inner circle that something was wrong with the People's Temple. Gossip surfaced that people were being held against their will. This prompted Jones to move the Temple to Guyana. The move added distance from critics, but did not stop the continued signs of trouble. The turmoil reached the ear of Leo Ryan, a California Congressman. He and some members of the state's media went to conduct a firsthand investigation. As they departed, several temple members indicated their wish to return with the investigators. After arriving at the airport they were ambushed by temple enforcers. Congressman Ryan, three members of the media, and one defector were killed; ten other members of the party were wounded.

Back at the temple, preparations were under way to enact for real the "white nights" ritual the group had practiced. Most voluntarily drank the fatal potion. Others were forced. Some were shot or shot themselves, including the group's founding wizard, the Reverend James Jones.

Jonestown in retrospect looks like a grisly perversion of the wizard's work of summoning and sustaining the human spirit. But some believers are still reluctant to let go of the magic and faith of the noble experiment. Laura Johnston Kohl, a Jonestown survivor, sums it up:

> Jonestown, to me, was heaven on earth. I really loved it. It was so exciting. I was drawn by the socialist political agenda rather than the religious part. Really, my interest was being in an integrated community. And it was. Unfortunately, Jim really went crazy. I didn't notice how bad he had gotten. Perhaps I was willing to overlook it. The rest of our life was fine. I was in Georgetown the day everything happened. If I had been there, I probably would have drunk the poisoned punch. At the time, I wasn't interested in returning to the life I had in the United States.[152]

Stephan Jones agrees: "There is one universal that attracted people to People's Temple—that deep desire to belong to something."[153]

LESSONS FROM TRAGEDY

In fiction and legend, destructive wizards—figures like Voldemort, Sauron, and the Wicked Witch of the East—are portrayed as incarnations of pure evil. It is comforting to view them as such, because we can blame them and deny our own shadows. Jim Jones seems to fit this view, at least in the last phase of his life, when noble purposes had transmuted to madness and megalomania. But reality is usually less clear-cut, as Andy Fastow's story illustrates. Fastow's character—his ambition, insecurity, and wobbly moral compass—put him at risk. Circumstances pushed him over the edge. To a degree, the same was true of Jim Jones, though he was much more the creator of his environment than Fastow was. If we ignore the circumstances, we will draw the simplistic conclusion that bad things happen because of evil people, devils who should be punished for their misdeeds.

While evil-doers deserve sanction, there is more to the story. Only by looking at the environmental factors that draw people into the harmful wizard role and then aid and abet them can we draw valid lessons from the Fastow and Jones stories.

1. *Harmful wizards are both villains and victims.*

Fastow's machinations crossed numerous ethical and legal lines and made Enron's crash almost inevitable. But Fastow's dark magic was not the only cause of the downfall. His opportunity to employ his financial shenanigans arose from a chronic problem at Enron: the company was perpetually short of cash. Many of its businesses weren't making enough money to support its image as an innovative, fast-growth enterprise. Lay and Skilling were obsessed with bolstering earnings to support a rising stock price. Their reputations and personal wealth depended on it. If the core businesses had been as profitable as Enron claimed, Fastow's dodgy SPEs wouldn't have been necessary. Fastow became indispensable to his bosses because he kept finding ways to generate bogus earnings. It was a mutual bargain with the devil.

With Jim Jones, the relationship between person and situation shifts. The individual takes the foreground, but circumstances still play a role. Jones belonged to a special group—prophetic charismatics. His fellows include individuals like Ron Hubbard (the founder of Scientology), David Koresh (leader of the Branch Davidians during the notorious stand-off at Waco, Texas), and Adolph Hitler. Prophetic charismatics typically grow up as wounded and lonely children. But they mature into adults who combine skills at empathy and manipulation with a vision of paradise. They have supreme confidence that they represent the ultimate good for their followers. They depend on the environment to supply a sufficient number of willing adherents whose unmet psychic and spiritual needs make them vulnerable to the charismatic's appeal. Sometimes, the disciples come to them (as happened for Adolph Hitler); sometimes they have to beat the bushes (as was true for Jim Jones).

Adolph Hitler's Nazi movement made little headway until the Depression created millions of scared and discouraged German citizens—just the audience Hitler needed. In his home state of Indiana, Jones had limited success in recruiting followers. But his movement soared when he relocated to San Francisco. Jones developed a message combining religion, a focus on eliminating racism and poverty, and a promise of unconditional love: "You'll never be loved again like I love you."[154] The City on the Bay in 1970 offered fertile ground for his appeal.

2. *Harmful wizards flourish in dark corners and ethical vacuums.*

A basic purpose of accounting rules is ensuring that a company presents an accurate and consistent picture of its economic health. But by the 1990s, those bookkeeping standards filled thousands of pages. "Interpreting them has always been more art than science, reliant in no small part on the good faith of those applying them in everyday situations. For very smart people who saw the rules as something to be gotten around, well, it wasn't all that hard to do."[155] For Enron people who prided themselves on being smarter than everyone, it was a real coup to exploit loopholes and push the rules to the limit. This was applauded in a company that valued the bottom line above all else. It was a toxic combination for an ambitious self-promoter and a culture that had become very effective at turning good people bad. "You could see the green MBAs coming in, so happy-go-lucky and innocent," said one Enron veteran. "Within six months, they'd become assholes."[156]

Much of the scheming could not have been sustained in the light of day. Fastow and his cohorts developed a conspiracy of positive spin and disclosed no more than they had to. Lay, Skilling, and the Enron board had all been informed about the major off-books deals, but they had asked few questions. As long as Fastow's tricks kept producing financial miracles when needed, his bosses had little incentive to look up the magician's sleeve.

Close oversight was a problem for Jim Jones as well. Although he was lionized by many community and political leaders during his early years in San Francisco, strange doings within the church began to attract increasing criticism. Recognizing that his movement could not survive in California, Jones decided to relocate to a rural area of the tiny nation of Guyana. That bought time, but the inquiry didn't end, and the visit by Congressman Ryan's delegation brought down the temple.

3. *Harmful wizards are never alone in their plots.*

Fastow was aided and abetted by a host of intentional or unintentional co-conspirators. His deals had to be approved by accountants, auditors, and his bosses. Some required Enron's board to exempt him from the company's ethics policy, which the board did with little discussion and few questions. Fastow's SPEs needed major funding from banks and investors, who were often well aware that they were treading on shaky ground. In one notorious example, Merrill Lynch agreed to buy three floating power plants off the coast of Nigeria, subject to Enron's unwritten promise to buy them back within six months. Both parties knew what the deal was about. Merrill Lynch had zero interest in owning offshore power assets, but Enron would get a short-term bump on its earnings. In return, the company would continue to steer deals in Merrill Lynch's direction. Some Merrill Lynch executives knew the deal stank, but they held their noses and marched ahead.

In short: a combination of personal impulses, Enron's culture, the 1990s business climate, and willing collaborators nudged Andrew Fastow into the role of harmful wizard. Once ensconced, his zeal and dark magic created a remarkable financial edifice. It was so impressive that Fastow won a national award for CFO excellence in 1999. But it was all built on the hope that Enron's stock would never fall and the company would always have the cash to bail itself out. When those assumptions crumbled, the shaky house of cards collapsed.

For Jones, co-conspirators were the elite members of his community, particularly the Planning Commission, a strange fusion of administrative rationality and nonstop encounter group. Its members did most of the administrative heavy lifting on Jones's behalf, enabling him to stay above the fray. They were well aware of his weaknesses and erratic mood swings, but nonetheless colluded with him to protect his image as "the only God you'll ever see."[157]

Consequently, the elite cadre not only promoted but believed strongly in their leader's charisma. They had faith that Jones did have magical power to heal, but that using this power exhausted him unduly, so that fakery was necessary to keep him alive. They believed in his Godlike qualities and were convinced that he could see the future, that he had information no one else possessed. These members also believed that the temple was the only antidote to all the ills of the world.[158]

4. *Harmful wizards suffer from their narrow field of view and create an alternate reality with the seeds of its own destruction.*

Fastow exemplifies characteristics often found in harmful wizards. He combined limited experience with a narrow focus on expanding his own power, reputation, and wealth. He was a securitization maven, but too young and inexperienced to be safe once given sufficient rope to hang both himself and his company. He didn't know how to be a chief financial officer, so he did what he knew—make deals. Encouraged by Enron's sense of itself as smarter and more creative than most other companies, he created a magical world in which the rules could be flouted or ignored and money grew on trees. The profits were mostly illusory, but that didn't prevent Fastow and many of his friends and business associates from taking huge windfalls—Enron's board was stunned to learn that Fastow had taken more than $40 million from two of the partnerships he had set up. For the young and ambitious: beware the boss or company who gives you more freedom than you can handle. The results may be catastrophic. They certainly were for Fastow and Enron, but also for Jim Jones.

Jones built his movement around a commitment to social justice and racial integration. He and most of his people seemed to believe they were creating a utopia that could solve the problems of poverty and injustice. As his church grew, Jones became more erratic, more demanding, and more convinced that the outside world wanted to destroy his noble effort. Loyalty tests intensified. Everyone was to confess error and be criticized for misdeeds—except him. Everyone was to toe the line and conform to a demanding code—which could change at any time according to his whim. Surrounded by followers who revered his power, believed in his fantasies, and catered to his whims, he and his inner cadre became increasingly disconnected from reality and any hope of recognizing the limits of his constricted focus.

The harmful wizard pattern is dismal and dismaying, but it offers important lessons. Seduced by their own flaws and by a supportive environment, harmful wizards become both villains and victims—destroying themselves and the institution or community they lead. They are abetted by co-conspirators who have needs of their own that the dark wizard can help them attain.

They flourish only when they can find a dark corner—a role that lets them operate with minimal scrutiny. The darkness prevents them from seeing the bigger picture and recognizing the potential harm of their misguided actions.

All this is avoidable. To escape the tragic fate of the harmful wizard, choose environments favorable to a strong moral compass. Find organizations that have a strong sense of identity and know and treasure what they value. Beware of co-conspirators—those who will ally themselves with you in service of their own selfish or narrow ends. Take on roles where your work is visible and provides regular opportunities for feedback. Choose situations that bring you in frequent contact with a range of people who bring diverse perspectives and preferences, and who will help you keep your wizardry authentic.

PART FIVE

WIZARDS AT WORK

Mary Kay Ash was tired of working for other people. She was a terrific salesperson who outperformed nearly all her colleagues. She was so good that she was often tapped to train other salespeople—mostly men. Once up to speed, many were promoted over her. That bothered her so much she decided to take a chance on her own and create her "dream company." Her venture was helped by a chance meeting with a woman who was selling cosmetics formulated by her father. Mary Kay bought the rights and put together a plan for a company that would market and sell the products. Her accountant warned her against the venture, cautioning that it was not economically viable. But Mary Kay had an ace in the hole—her husband had a knack for the operational details of a new enterprise.

As Mary Kay and her husband were going over the final details before launching the new business, he suffered a fatal heart attack. She turned to her accountant and attorney for counsel. Their advice: pull the plug and recoup whatever you can. But Mary Kay was determined to go on, bolstered by the echo of her mother's encouraging words: "You can do it."

Mary Kay Cosmetics was launched as a company devoted to giving women a chance to succeed. It was a business built more than anything else on May Kay Ash's faith in herself and in women like her. Very few hard-core businesspeople shared her faith, but she believed that the bottom line would take care of itself if the usual emphasis on "P&L" was redefined as "People and Love." She was also convinced that public recognition for a job well done was the wellspring of motivation. The company quickly became known for its frequent rituals and lavish annual celebrations. These events were resplendent with symbols that expressed and defined the "Mary Kay way." Her experience led Mary Kay to believe that the best symbols were both beautiful and useful:

> At Mary Kay, we gained international attention for "symbols" such as automobiles, furs, dream vacations, and diamonds. But it all began with something I called the Golden Goblet Club. My intent was simple enough: for each monthly wholesale transaction of $1000, a Consultant would win a beautiful, gold-plated goblet. . . . Only a few people will own a golden goblet, and they'll do it because they want the recognition the goblet symbolizes.[159]

At her death, Mary Kay was chairman emeritus of a multibil-lion-dollar company. Her magic had created hundreds of female mil-lionaires. Her legacy was an enterprise devoted as much to providing economic and spiritual opportunities for women as to maintaining a healthy bottom line.

Howard Schultz's story is a different version of a kindred theme. Schultz grew up in a crowded housing project in Brooklyn, New York. His working-class parents were financially strapped, and he had to work many jobs at an early age. Even with his contributions to the family's coffers, money was always tight. Coffee played only a minor role in Schultz's childhood. His mother drank instant coffee. When company came she would buy a pound of canned coffee and stoke up an old percolator. That occasional ritual stuck with Schultz: "I remem-ber listening to [the percolator] grumble and watching that little glass cap until finally the coffee popped into it like a jumping bean."[160]

After working his way through college, Schultz migrated from job to job. He worked for Xerox making fifty cold calls a day and then moved to a Swedish firm where he was promoted to vice presi-dent in charge of their housewares business. He performed well and rose quickly, but something basic was missing—passion. Then fate intervened for him in the same way it had for Ray Kroc. Kroc had gone west to check out a hamburger stand named McDonald's because it was buying so many of his milkshake machines. Schultz traveled west to find out why a little company in Seattle called Star-bucks was a huge buyer of a low-tech coffee maker. He found his bliss in his first cup of Starbucks coffee:

> The counterman scooped out some Sumatra coffee beans, ground them, put the grounds in a filter in the cone, and poured hot water over them. Although the task took only a few minutes, he approached the work almost reverently, like an artisan. . . . When he handed me a porcelain mug filled with that freshly brewed coffee, the steam and aroma seemed to envelop my entire face. There was no question of adding milk or sugar. I took a small tentative sip. . . . *Whoa.* I threw

my head back and my eyes shot wide open. Even from a single sip, I could tell it was stronger than any coffee I had ever tasted. . . . By the third sip, I was hooked.[161]

Later that day, he met with the Starbucks founders to discuss the ins and outs of the specialty coffee business. They had an exciting meeting of the minds about quality and offering a product well ahead of expectations to raise the sophistication of customers' tastes. That meeting got Schultz hooked on the company as well as the product. He decided to join up. The Starbucks owners were successful and passionate about their business, but were content to offer the best coffee beans in the Seattle market. Schultz gave Starbucks what Ray Kroc had brought to McDonald's years earlier—imagination and a vision that went well beyond a hometown retail operation.

Serendipity intervened once more on a trip to Italy. Schultz fell in love with the espresso bars that seemed to be on every corner and with a drink he'd never tasted before—*caffè e latte*. He came back to Seattle convinced that America needed espresso bars, only to find himself in a long-running debate with his boss, who believed that the business was beans, not beverages. Eventually, Schultz resolved the debate by doing what Kroc did—purchasing the business. On the day of the purchase, he held an all-hands meeting at the old Starbucks roasting plant. He had just three talking points: "1. Speak from my heart. 2. Put myself in their shoes. 3. Share the Big Dream with them."[162]

By 2000, Starbucks had become an international business with revenues over one billion dollars. Even more important, Schultz has been able to instill in employees the reverence for the coffee experience he encountered in the Starbucks *barista* who brewed him his first cup. This same spirit permeates Starbucks coffee bars today:

A company can grow big without losing the passion and personality that built it, but only if it's driven not by profits but by people. . . .

The key is heart. I pour my heart into every cup of coffee and so do my partners at Starbucks. When customers sense that, they respond in kind. . . . If you pour your heart into your work, you can achieve dreams others may think impossible. That's what makes life rewarding.[163]

Both Howard Schultz and Mary Kay Ash have waved a magic wand to create organizations that inspire both people inside and those on the outside who long for something that arouses passion and gives work and life meaning. These two leaders understood the role of legendary wizards like Merlin. As legend has it, Merlin was born in the future and moved backward in time to the past. His ideas were often out of step and ahead of their time because he could foresee what lay ahead. Charles Smith has likened successful executives to legendary wizards: "Exceptional leaders cultivate the Merlin-like habit of acting in the present moment as ambassadors of a radically different future, in order to imbue their organizations with a breakthrough vision of what is possible to achieve."[164]

Ash and Schultz did not start as wizards. They evolved through their individual odysseys. Each was on a pilgrimage in search of passion and something to believe in long before they knew what the brass ring would look like. Both learned from experience, successes as well as frustrations, and both were ready when luck or fate opened up a new possibility. Only then were they able to develop an image of a transforming reality. Both faced skepticism but were fueled by their passion and courage, and they were both sustained by an abiding faith in their chosen pursuit. One of the clearest lessons from their stories is that magic can be learned and wizardry can be cultivated. The following chapters discuss how. Chapter Thirteen delves into the world of magic and the concept of soul. Chapter Fourteen identifies the ways of wizards—stories, ritual and ceremony, and icons, their mediums for creating meaningful places of work.

13

THE WIZARD'S ODYSSEY

"Can't you give me brains?" asked the Scarecrow.

"You don't need them. You are learning something every day. A baby has brains, but it doesn't know much. Experience is the only thing that brings knowledge, and the longer you are on the earth the more experience you are sure to get."

"That may all be true," said the Scarecrow, "but I shall be very unhappy unless you give me brains."

—L. FRANK BAUM[165]

Modern managers are often as stubborn as the scarecrow, insisting that someone give them what they already have. They want their heads stuffed with knowledge and a diploma to hang on the wall, forgetting that wisdom comes from experience. "Wisdom is the ability to make correct judgments and decisions. It is an intangible quality gained through experience. Whether or not something is wise is determined in a pragmatic sense by its popularity, how long it has been around, and its ability to predict against future events."[166]

Another way to capture the essence of wisdom is offered by Joseph Meeker: "[Wisdom] is an awareness of wholeness that does not lose sight of particularity or concreteness, or of the intricacies of interrelationships. It is where left and right brain come together in a union of logic and poetry and sensation, and where self-awareness is no longer at odds with awareness of the otherness of the world. Wisdom . . . is the consciousness of wholeness and integrity that transcends both. Wisdom is complexity understood and relationships accepted."[167]

1. *Wizards are wise.*

They share the sentiment of Alfred Lord Tennyson, "Knowledge comes but wisdom lingers." But attaining wisdom is not a passive process. Experience provides the raw material. Reflection gleans the important enduring lessons. Too many leaders are so riveted to specific goals that they overlook promising new ideas or directions and too anchored in details to see the forest beyond the trees. Here's a fable that illustrates the point:

An old sage was walking along a forest path. Another man, much younger, approached from the other direction. The young man's eyes were so riveted to the path that he bumped into the sage. The sage looked at the young man sternly and asked him where he was going. "To catch my future," the young man replied. "How do you know you haven't already passed it?" the sage asked.

Wizards are deeply immersed in day-to-day events while simultaneously looking on with the keen eye of a detached observer. Heifetz and Linsky call it "the ability to move back and forth between the dance floor and the balcony."[168] Wizards are able to separate the profound from the mundane and to weave past, present, and future into an integrated web. This provides the wisdom they then can share with others, not so much by offering specific advice but by asking questions, using metaphors, and telling stories to guide leaders to what they have missed or already know. Wizards rely on uncommon common sense, distilled from life's ongoing ups and downs.

2. *Wizards embrace foibles and folly.*

Avoiding mistakes or trying to cover them up produces a large share of the errors and toxicity we often see in organizations and societies. Fear of error kills creativity and innovation. Concealing bungled situations has created havoc in the highest levels of our government. Presidents Nixon, Reagan, and Clinton all dug themselves into holes by trying to gloss over lapses of judgment. With greater wisdom, they could have acknowledged fault in the beginning and avoided much pain down the road. Jerry Ortiz y Pino put a more wizardly spin on mistakes in his *Santa Fe Reporter* column: "Wisdom . . . only comes from living, from making mistakes—or from listening to others who have made mistakes and learned from them."[169]

Wizards view mistakes as opportunities for learning and growth. The bigger the blunder, the greater the possibilities. A story from Southwest Airlines illustrates the point. A company executive, Matt Buckley, came up with a novel idea for increasing the airline's revenue stream: create a delivery service faster than FedEx—same-day delivery under the label "Rush Plus." Southwest could do it because it had many more flights every day than the competition. The idea was sold to CEO Herb Kelleher and Southwest's board, who made a sizable investment in the new service. The problem was that customers stayed away, which made it an expensive blooper. After the failure, Buckley felt like hiding in a cave to escape the torrent of Rush Plus jokes flowing from his colleagues. But then he realized something: "The more I was exposed to the jokes and jabs, the better I felt. People were actually trying to help me heal."[170] Instead of being fired as he feared, he got promoted—repeatedly.

A wizard's take on mistakes also recognizes that many scientific and corporate innovations were unplanned surprises. 3M's highly profitable Post-it notes were the result of a failed adhesive formulated by an employee. Procter & Gamble's classic Ivory Soap floated because a batch was accidentally over-aerated. To be sure, errors can be very expensive. But emphasizing blame rather than lessons learned results in the same foibles and follies repeating over and over again. It also encourages people to avoid risks, thereby damaging growth and performance.

3. *Wizards are intimately connected with soul.*

A treasure trove of spiritual enlightenment nestles deep within the human soul. Soul is special and unique, grounded in the substrata of personal experience. But it also is a repository of cumulative wisdom passed on through cosmic osmosis. Soul is our core, our mystical center—inherited at birth, enriched as we live, and passed on when we die. The Persian poet Rumi expresses it this way:

> *All day I think about it, then at night I say it.*
>
> *Where did I come from,*
>
> *And what am I supposed to be doing?*
>
> *I have no idea.*
>
> *My soul is from elsewhere, I'm sure of that,*
>
> *And I intend to end up there.*[171]

Wizards probe within their souls to navigate life's peaks and valleys. In the film *Wall Street,* Martin Sheen's character delivers a powerful line: "Man looks into an abyss. There is nothing staring back at him. At that moment, the man discovers his character. And that is what keeps him out of the abyss." Character, or soul, is a moral compass that points to the right direction in the absence of other clues. Curnow identifies a sage (that is, a wizard) as "an individual with a highly developed sense of ethical intuition . . . the sage can be relied upon to act appropriately in any situation."[172]

In the early 1980s James Burke, then CEO of Johnson & Johnson (J&J), faced a daunting predicament. Someone had laced bottles of Tylenol with cyanide, causing seven deaths in the Chicago area. Initially, no one knew the extent of the incident. Was it a localized event or a much broader problem? Pulling the product from outlets across the country would be a huge financial blow to the company. But what if a tainted bottle resulted in more deaths elsewhere? Faced with a quandary, Burke made the ethical choice. J&J recalled every bottle of Tylenol in America, and restocked only after taking the time to develop tamper-proof packaging. Burke's decision honored and reinforced the soul of J&J—customer health comes ahead of shareholders and any other interests.

Wounds, crises, and dramatic encounters often connect us to our inner core, forcing us to ask what really matters. For what are we willing to sacrifice? Civil rights workers were willing to go to jail to advance the cause of freedom. Soldiers are willing to die for their country. Businesspeople also extract potent schooling from harrowing experiences. The CEO of a large Canadian corporation was driving home from a dinner party accompanied by his wife and daughter. It was a typical winter evening in Toronto—cold, misty, and icy. As they crossed some railroad tracks, their car slipped on the ice and got stuck. The wife yelled at her husband: "There's a train coming!" He saw the lights of the locomotive bearing down. He yelled for his wife to run. Then he tried to pull his daughter from the back of the car. Her foot was wedged under the front seat. As he pulled, the train drew dangerously close. He then made a pledge to himself: I'm going to stay and die with her." At the last minute, he was able to pull her out. They escaped just as the train demolished the family car.

Later the executive reflected on the close call: "That night changed my life. I came to grips with what is sacred to me. Now my relationship with my family is much closer. I am a totally different boss at work. I realize that people come first. My company has become a warm and wonderful place to work. As an unintended benefit, our performance has nearly doubled."[173]

Soulful organizations today are few and far between. For more than a decade, one exception was Saturn Motors, officially "The car company with a soul." Saturn was founded in the early 1980s as an effort by General Motors to do an end-run around the company's usual operations, which were then producing some of the most poorly built automobiles on the road. A "Gang of 100," composed of representatives from all relevant groups—including the union—was charged with surveying exemplary business practices worldwide and distilling them into a philosophy tailor-made for a unique approach to automobile manufacturing. The result drew out the best from auto-workers who had been shackled by the top-down practices of Detroit. They proved that a different kind of company could produce a different kind of car. Saturn's first cars came off the assembly line in 1990, and immediately began winning awards for quality and performance. Innovating in everything from employee relations to dealer sales practices, the new company captured the hearts of a loyal group of customers. Sadly, the noble experiment came to a close in 2005 when General Motors closed the Spring Hill plant as part of a massive cut-back. Still, the company proved what can be done if people are given a chance to create a meaningful and spirited work environment.

4. *Wizards are magical.*

In the classic movie *Miracle on 34th Street*, an older gentleman of questionable sanity is put on trial because he publicly claims to be Santa Claus. Fred, a young trial lawyer, agrees to defend "Kris Kringle" in a competency hearing where the prosecution argues that he is crazy and needs to be institutionalized. Fred stuns the court, arguing that Kringle is actually Santa Claus and he intends to prove it. After the initial hearing, Fred visits his fiancé, who takes a dim view of Fred's quixotic quest. She is particularly worried because Fred's law firm has fired him, thereby jeopardizing their future plans. He asks if she believes in him. She responds that it is just a matter of common sense. He counters, "Faith is believing in things when common sense tells you not to." She accuses him of "acting like a child" and says that he's "living in a realistic world where lovely intangibles are attractive but don't matter very much. That's not the way you get ahead." Fred responds that it depends on your definition of getting ahead. He closes the argument by saying: "Look Doris, you are going to find out someday that your way of facing this realistic world doesn't work. And when you do, don't overlook those lovely little intangibles. You'll discover that they are the only things that are worthwhile."

Miracle on 34th Street is an old film that addresses an enduring issue: which is more important in life and work: memos or magic, policies or poetry? We relish the times when we feel the spirit and cherish the awe and enchantment of magical moments. The celebration of the winter solstice, for example, takes different forms across the world at the darkest days of the year. From a religious perspective this magical time celebrates treasured values, showcases unifying symbols, and revisits unique stories. Yet some argue, as does Daniel O'Keefe in *Stolen Lightning*, "It is magic and ourselves that we love in Christmas, not religion or god."[174]

In our modern, scientific world we have jettisoned magic. We disparage it with terms like voodoo, sleight of hand, hocus pocus, trickery. Magic has been replaced in most organizations by facts, figures, and technology. But deep down it is still the allure of magic that we yearn for in our life and work:

> Magic has not its origin in fraud. . . . Its roots lie much deeper than any conscious purpose . . . [in] the human need for expressing such ideas. Whatever purpose magical practice may serve, its direct motivation is the desire to symbolize great conceptions. The power of conception—of "having ideas"—is man's peculiar asset, and awareness of this power is an exciting sense of human strength.
>
> Nothing is more thrilling than the dawn of a new conception. The symbols that embody ideas of life and death, of man and the word, are naturally sacred.[175]

From this perspective, magic builds confidence in situations of uncertainty. Magical actions also create or transform the ordinary into something special. Take, for example, Hewlett-Packard and the well-known and highly touted HP way. Former CEO John Young has described it as "just a magical formula."[176]

How magic produces social effects and links actions to consequences is typically shrouded in mystery. One definition of a magician is someone who produces effects in ways the rest of us cannot comprehend or explain. But if we look at many examples of magic that we see in groups and organizations, we often see that its essence is transforming the ordinary into the extraordinary. Winter, with its long nights and miserable weather, gets depressing, but then along comes a holiday with its lights, celebrations, and festive events to restore our spirits. Selling electronic gadgets may become humdrum at times, but a cultural anchor like the HP way gives a corporation the feeling of specialness and community. Selling cosmetics to neighbors is scary, but receiving a diamond bumblebee in front of an audience of 5,000 colleagues is magical. Finding magic is as easy as looking for comparable possibilities. They're there, and only those who look will find them. Magic is one of the essential tasks of wizards. Like most symbolic forms and actions, the value and impact of magic in contemporary organizations is a matter of belief and faith. These crucial ingredients are essential to group cohesion and top performance.

5. *Wizardry is within reach.*

Most of us devote more time than we realize searching for someone to wave a wand and solve our problems or infuse our lives with meaning and purpose. We visit psychiatrists. We join clubs and cults. We devour the latest writings of a multitude of self-help gurus. We hire high-priced consultants. We look outside ourselves, hoping to find someone or something that will restore the enchantment of childhood—before we were told that Santa Claus and the Tooth Fairy didn't exist. They were fictions that we now should outgrow.

Magic had to be carefully bounded, confined to an occasional visit to a magical world such as Disneyland.

In our relentless search for wizards, we overlook a prime source—our own souls. Baum's classic tale got it right a long time ago. When the Great Oz was exposed, he was not an all-seeing, commanding being. He was a little old man with a wrinkled face and a bald head. His power was based on deception and trickery. He was omniscient and omnipotent only because others believed him to be. After discovering the reality behind the façade when Oz confessed to "making believe" rather than practicing real magic, Dorothy was disappointed and angry:

> "Making believe!" cried Dorothy. "Are you not a great wizard?"
>
> "Hush, my dear," he said. "Don't speak so loud, or you will be overheard—and I should be ruined. I'm supposed to be a Great Wizard."
>
> "And aren't you?" she asked.
>
> "Not a bit of it, my dear; I'm just a common man."[177]

Baum's story teaches that the power of wizardry is inside each of us. We have common sense or wisdom that can be unleashed if we stop looking outside and focus instead on our inner journey. In story and legend, the odyssey takes us through three stages to arrive at our inner core. The first is leaving home psychically and spiritually. This requires letting go of familiar ways and escaping the shackles of established convention and daily routine. Mary Kay Ash unmoored herself from a corporate job and a steady paycheck. Howard Schultz moved from New York to Seattle to find his dream. The second stage of the journey is a perilous quest or venturesome pilgrimage to seek a subterranean level of human awareness. As Joseph Campbell writes: "The dark night of the soul comes just before the revelation. When everything is lost, and all seems darkness, then comes the new life."[178]

The dark night is terrifying but indispensable. Only after that can we embark on the third stage of the journey—returning home, armed with new capacities and a deeper understanding of who we are and what we can do to enrich the lives of others. Now the wizard can go to work and inspired leadership begins.

14

SUMMONING
THE SPIRIT

*The freedom that we provide to the American people, the freedom to fly, is
really the idealistic and ennobling purpose of Southwest Airlines and all of
its wonderful people. Just as a bricklayer is not just laying bricks, with each
brick he lays he is building a home, so too are our people not just answering
phones or throwing bags or collecting tickets or maintaining airplanes. We
are, each of us as we do these things each day, giving people the freedom to
fly; the great service of freedom that you, the people of Southwest Airlines,
provide to the people of America is indeed the higher calling and the
greater cause that each of us answers each day when we come to work. . . .
No other airline brings so much to so many and I thank you for doing that.*

—HERB KELLEHER[179]

As CEO of Southwest, Kelleher used these words to launch the
company's Freedom to Fly campaign. Before Southwest, only the
affluent could afford air travel. If individuals of limited means
wanted to hold a new grandchild, comfort a dying friend, attend

a graduation, or be present at a bas mitzvah, their only travel options were car or bus. Southwest changed that and multiplied the number of passengers winging their way to destinations across America.

To Southwest employees, whatever their jobs, work has meaning beyond a simple economic transaction. Matthew Fox puts this in a broader spiritual context:

> Life and livelihood ought not to be separated but to flow from the same source, which is Spirit, for both life and livelihood are about Spirit. Spirit means life, and both life and livelihood are about living in depth, living with meaning, purpose, joy, and a sense of contributing to the greater community. A spirituality of work is about bringing life and livelihood back together again, And Spirit with them.[180]

Southwest oozes spirit. It bonds employees together in an uncommon quest. It captures the hearts of customers, who become players in the otherwise no-frills company's fun. It shows in day-to-day operations. It shows up on the bottom line. For years, Southwest has been one of America's most profitable air carriers.

Herb Kelleher, Southwest's co-founder and long-time CEO, played a central role in its success. His fun-loving, self-deprecating wizardry was contagious. Kelleher would go to any lengths to dramatize Southwest's values. Robert Crandall, American Airlines' former CEO, once joshed Kelleher about painting an aircraft in the likeness of Shamu the whale by asking, "What are you going to do with all that whale shit?" Kelleher promptly sent a huge tub of chocolate mousse to American's Dallas headquarters.

When Southwest unknowingly purloined the slogan "just plane smart" from tiny Stevens Aviation, Kelleher immediately accepted a challenge from Stevens's CEO, Kurt Herwald, to skip litigation and arm wrestle for the rights. They rented an arena in Dallas and filled it with a capacity crowd of employees from both companies. As an avid weight trainer, Herwald had an overwhelming edge over the chain-smoking, heavy-drinking Kelleher. The outcome was never in doubt, but the fix was in. After Herwald's quick victory, he announced Stevens was giving Southwest permission to use the slogan. The slogan battle was one of many occasions that reinforced one of Southwest's core beliefs: fun is not a four-letter word, fear is.

Like Mother Teresa and Richard Nixon, Kelleher had his shadow. His well-known fondness for bourbon and his three-pack-a-day smoking habit were a poor recipe for great health. His public utterances sometimes bordered on crassness. On National Public Radio's *Press Club,* he was asked to share his most noteworthy accomplishments. His response: "Projectile vomiting, and I've never had a real serious venereal disease." But that was all part of what made Kelleher loveable: he made no apologies for his shadow. He dismissed concerns about his cigarette habit because "I have floppy veins and smoking firms them up." He was authentic and comfortable being himself. But along with his happy-go-lucky public persona, he was deeply committed to the abiding ideals of Southwest Airlines and was not afraid of reinforcing this moral code in an emotional, almost religious way.

Kelleher's role in embodying and cultivating the airline's spirit is remarkable. But equally admirable is the contribution of many others in nourishing the culture. Colleen Barrett, Kelleher's second-in-command who became president, is just as passionate and talented in projecting and preserving the special qualities that have captured the hearts of both employees and customers. A cultural committee composed of representatives across different functions monitors how well the company lives up to its espoused values. Even more important, countless unofficial wizards sprinkled at all levels work to keep the spirit alive. It's not just the big cheeses at the top who regularly reinforce values, preside over rituals, convene celebrations, and tell stories.

It's a community responsibility. Leadership is dispersed. As Colleen Barrett admits, the secret to Southwest's success is no secret. It's people, unified around a higher calling and noble purpose, who make the company tick.

Spirit is there to be summoned and maintained in any group. It just takes someone to release it. The magic formula centers on values, icons, ritual, ceremony, and stories. The elements of that elixir are available to anyone, anywhere. But someone has to ignite the wizard within and take the risk to make the chemistry work.

1. *Values unify purpose, focus, and behavior.*

A peek beneath the surface of almost any high-performing organization brings into bold relief a set of widely shared conventions and beliefs.[181] People do the right thing because it is deeply ingrained, not because it is formally dictated. Values set a higher moral code, which is often articulated during the hiring process. A candidate for a management position at Wal-Mart was asked during her interview if she would like a cup of coffee. She responded affirmatively and was directed to a coffee machine where she could purchase a cup for twenty-five cents. At the end of the interview, she was shown a table of mementos. For a price, she could take home souvenirs of her visit. The message: at Wal-Mart we are dedicated to keeping costs down.

New employees at Nordstrom Department Stores are handed a card labeled "Company Handbook." Rule number 1 states: "Use your best judgment in all situations. There will be no additional rules."[182] The message: we put a premium on customer service and rely on your sound judgment to make it happen. The values of FedEx are succinctly articulated in the company's philosophy: People, Service, and Profits . . . in that order. That is one reason customers trust FedEx to deliver their parcels.

When values are internalized and shared, an organization doesn't need a wordy mission statement or tight supervision. People go about their work with the same end in mind, heart, and soul. If people deviate from the chosen path, informal peer pressure quickly brings them back on track. Everyone, even the top dogs, conforms to the same code of ethical behavior.

2. *Icons and emblems shape abstract values into vivid representations.*

Condensing intangible values into accessible prose is difficult. At some point, organizations need to create icons and emblems that convey a bedrock sense of identity to insiders and outsiders. The emblems of the Red Cross or Red Crescent, Nike's Swoosh, Target's red bull's eye, and McDonald's Golden Arches are examples of cultural branding. The images serve as emotional rallying points to make spirit manifest. In America and most other nations, citizens salute the flag, sing the national anthem, and devise penalties for acts of desecration that trample on what the flag represents. Honoring the flag draws citizens together in spiritual union. When competing values arise, their adherents create alternative images, such as the peace symbol that signified opposition to the Vietnam War.

People develop strong emotional attachments to icons and emblems. When these are questioned or attacked, people will defend the icon or attack its enemies. For example, at one seminar devoted to examining the influence of culture in federal agencies, a representative from what was then called the General Accounting Office (GAO) pooh-poohed symbols as being hollow and frivolous. An executive from the U.S. Forest Service asked him if his critique applied to Smokey the Bear. The GAO manager said yes. The Forest Service executive turned bright red and stormed out the door. He returned with a Smokey the Bear pin, thrust it into the hand of the critic, and then gave him the finger.[183] Gangs mark their territories with signs, the act of tagging. If a competing gang puts their sign over someone else's, it may trigger all-out war. Icons and emblems cut deeply into the human psyche.

Replacing or altering icons ruptures symbolic attachments and pushes people into depression or goads them into action. The Coca-Cola Company's decision to replace original Coke was based on taste tests that clearly showed people liked a new formula better. New Coke was then launched as a replacement for the original, which had been concocted in Atlanta a century earlier. Consumers howled. Employees were appalled. The din was so deafening and sales were so weak that management did an immediate retreat and restored the old recipe as Classic Coke. Put very simply, people don't like their cherished icons and emblems to be messed with. Doing so disrupts cherished rituals, threatens identity, and undercuts the human spirit.

3. *Rituals bond people to each other and reinforce the sense of community.*

We devote much of our energy on a daily basis to reaching a goal or accomplishing a task. Particularly at work we are judged on what we produce. This often leaves little time for activities that connect us to colleagues and community. We rarely get reminders of deeper purposes, the hard-to-articulate reasons why we work. Ritual fills the spiritual void we too often feel on the job. Matthew Fox describes it eloquently: "Ritual is an indispensable element for authentic community because in it we come together to name and celebrate, to lament, grieve, and let go, and to create and recreate our common task: the Great Work of the universe."[184]

In business, rituals also play a vital symbolic role. The H.B. Fuller Company produces adhesives of all kinds. The company takes pride in its ability to create new products and manufacturing processes and in its exemplary safety record. These two values are kept foremost in people's minds by a ritual at the beginning of all meetings: five minutes on innovation and five minutes on safety.

Internet giant eBay is built on two core values: commerce and community. It has fended off competitors and become the world's largest Internet auction business largely because of its spiritual commitment to bringing people together and connecting them with one another. Founder Pierre Omidyar is soulful about the company's purpose. "What we are doing here is building a place where people can come together. They just happen to be coming together around trading."[185]

Community at eBay is fostered, in large part, through a variety of rituals. One of eBay's most sacred elements is its feedback system to rate buyers and sellers. Those who have never traded on eBay would probably find it hard to fathom the emotional intensity around such issues as "leaving a negative," or the rage expressed at those who try to game the system. Other rituals have evolved around the many interactive discussion opportunities on eBay's Web site. There is a tradition called TUZ (an artificial acronym for a series of numeral 2's, in homage to the geeky initiator who made it a point to post a message on 2/22 at exactly 22:22:22, eBay time, purely for the fun of it). A TUZ Web site, designed by a user, features a TUZ history, hall of fame, and a list of birthdays of regular TUZ participants. Elsewhere on eBay, regular Friday night "sing alongs" give users a chance to post their favorite seventies song lyrics on the message board. The Elvis chat board has a virtual celebration of his birthday every January 8, complete with digital photos of birthday cakes. The rituals help to keep "the heart of the eBay community" beating.[186] Omidyar is a wizard who realizes the importance of ritual in summoning and sustaining the collective spirit.

Ritual prepares us for "Great Work." Surgeons scrub for seven minutes before a procedure, aware that modern germicides destroy bacteria in thirty seconds. Before takeoff, the first officer on a commercial flight walks around the aircraft for a last-minute inspection, knowing there is little chance of spotting a problem. In each case, the ritual is a reminder of and preparation for the awesome responsibility for preserving and protecting human life.

Rituals are crucial in any circumstances that combine high stakes with high uncertainty, such as preparations for combat in the military. Without ritual, warriors have trouble developing the right mind-set— a willingness to kill or be killed—and then making the transition back to a noncombat mode. A colonel at the Air War College puts it this way: "We have to collectively flip a switch going into battle and then reset it coming out. That was our trouble in Vietnam; we never really flipped the switch together."[187] For fighter pilots ritual is especially important:

> For me, there can be no fighter pilots without fighter pilot ritual. The end result of these rituals is a culture that allows individuals to risk their lives and revel in it. If the normal American finds it difficult to understand the circumstances that compel an individual to willingly hurtle their body through space encased in several tons of steel while determined people are actively trying to kill them, it is because the normal American has not been indoctrinated into the fighter pilot culture.[188]

The fighter pilot's world is encased in ritual. Ritual that recognizes accomplishments. Ritual that softens grief and heals wounds. Fun rituals. Rituals that govern key relationships. These rituals sustain fighter pilots.

4. *Ceremony beckons the spirit.*

Ceremony is one of the most powerful ways that groups and organizations connect to their history, communicate and celebrate values, build bonds among members, and deepen a sense of identity. Great organizations understand this. Home Depot's founders, Bernie Marcus and Arthur Blank, built their business on customer service and merchandise selection. With more than fifteen hundred stores, they can't greet every customer, but they know the experience they want every customer to have. Ceremony plays a key role in their tireless effort to ensure that every Home Depot employee is dedicated to making sure that customers find what they want and get the help they need.

At 6:30 A.M. on a typical August Sunday, no Home Depot stores were open, but Marcus and Blank were already working the crowd in a tent outside a store in Atlanta. The audience was mostly employees—

some with orange face paint, others shaking orange pom-poms, all wearing authentic Home Depot orange aprons.

They're all there for a television show, *Breakfast with Bernie and Arthur,* aimed exclusively at Home Depot employees. It's playful and often funny, but above all it's a chance for the founders to connect to their people, build bonds, remind them of what Home Depot is all about, and inform them about important news. When Marcus and Blank come in, clad in matching polo shirts and orange aprons, the crowd cheers enthusiastically. Blank gives Marcus a kiss on the cheek and the crowd cheers some more. Marcus and Blank open their show withy poignant stories of special employees:

> A mentally retarded worker in a California store cleans bathrooms and sweeps floors. "He's just a great asset to us," says his store manager. "He doesn't shy back from anything." A Jacksonville, Florida, employee has developed a Home Depot coloring book for children. And a Home Depot employee who fell out of a tree and broke his neck, partially paralyzing himself, is recovering. "We are waiting diligently for you to get back," says Marcus to the employee, Chris Owens, who is in the tent. "We love you, and you're one of our family." He then turns to the crowd and says, "You work for this company and you know you've got tremendous support." These examples show that while Marcus and Blank are about to go out of their way to help a handful of special employees, they are also assisting and praising other workers.
>
> Marcus and Blank are now ready to show how far they will go for their employees. "These stories very much remind me of the Olympics," says Blank to the crowd. "There's a lot of similarities between the spirit of the Olympics and our employees." Adds Marcus: "It's a lot like what Home Depot is doing. We're going to continue the best service. We've got to be dedicated in the same way. We have to reach our goals."[189]

Such ceremonial gatherings are common in Home Depot's "Bleeding Orange" culture. The rally-like atmosphere rouses the company's shared spirit. It takes everyone beyond the routine, creating a special time for Marcus and Blank, the company wizards, to put cultural values on dramatic display. Stories of employees overcoming difficulties underscore the family atmosphere Home Depot fosters. Stories of people going out of their way to assist customers exemplify the excellent service the company is known for. Stories of people helping out in the local community convey the outreach efforts Marcus and Blank encourage. The ceremony provides an emotionally charged place to anoint and appreciate heroes and heroines. Honoring heroic employees and their exploits provides concrete exemplars and encourages others to aspire to the same high standards.

Marcus and Blank themselves model what they expect from others in a highly visible public exhibit. The color orange is everywhere, especially in the aprons that are the official cultural costumes. The event might seem zany and frivolous to outsiders, but it makes sense to employees. Such occasions, along with many other special milestones, coalesce into the symbolic glue that has made Home Depot so successful.

Celebrations serve many purposes and take on many different emotional colorations. Some are as energetic and fun-filled as Home Depot's. Others are more solemn and poignant. Hawaii is renowned for its contagious Aloha spirit. Tourists are quickly caught up in the mystique and often act in ways they seldom do back home. But Aloha spirit dissipates on their return to cultures far less playful and earthy than the island paradise they left behind.

To the *kamaainas* (locals), the Aloha spirit has a deeper, historically rooted meaning that undergirds unique symbolic ways. In the early 1800s, Hawaiian cultural practices and beliefs were undermined by the impact and influence of western civilization. Exploits of explorers and adventurers led, in 1819, to the overthrow of the *kapu* system, a traditional set of laws (*kanawai*, or rules) and taboos (*kapu*, or prohibitions and privileges) central to Hawaiians' social, spiritual, and political values and stability. By the 1820s, American missionaries further demoralized Hawaiians with the destruction of the *heiaus* (temples), which were central to Hawaiian religious beliefs and cultural rituals. Laws forbade the public display of *hula* (dance) and *oli* (chant) essential to the oral history of the Hawaiian culture. Those who violated these prohibitions were subject to monetary fines and imprisonment. "For Hawaiians, the loss of power and rights in their homeland was tantamount to losing their sense of purpose and identity. Hawaiian epistemology often lost relevance amid modernization and industrialization that spelled the end of a subsistence economy and associated life-ways."[190]

The native Hawaiian essence—language, history, traditions, rituals, ceremonies—became almost dormant, kept alive by a few deeply committed souls. More recently, there has been a significant movement to revive and rekindle the roots of the Aloha spirit. Hawaiians call this "a 'Ho'oulu', a time of growth, hope and spirit."[191] This revisiting of what it means to be Hawaiian was launched with an extravagant cultural ceremony, reenacting the unification of the islands and the two hundredth anniversary of the completion of King Kamehameha's *heiau*, or temple of state. As one of the event's leaders described the purpose of the gathering: "All this is symbolic and yet symbols are what we live by, all cultures do. It's about reviving what was put on hold, bringing it back one more time and moving forward."[192]

Hundreds of Hawaiians took part in the ceremonial pageantry. They wore traditional costumes that they made themselves using age-old methods. They performed ancient rituals learned from island elders. Kahunas (priests) chanted haunting traditional chants. Figures of primeval gods presided over a ritual sacrifice. Toward the ceremony's dramatic close, representatives from other Polynesian islands chanted, danced, and brought symbols from their cultures to cement time-honored ties with the Hawaiians. Both participants and spectators were emotionally and spiritually drawn into the celebration of their heritage. Their voices speak to the power of the event:

"I'm not doing this because it is a show; I'm doing it because it is part of me."

"You don't know what to expect. You know it is going to be an interesting experience but I didn't realize it would sink so deeply into my gut."

"The experience was overwhelming. It moves something inside me emotionally that I can't comprehend sometimes."

"I thought it would be just a gathering, a one-day event, but as it turned out it is for the rest of my life and for my children's lives."

"I don't know that it changed my life. It became [my life] . . ."

"It made our heritage tangible, the thing we pass on to one another."

Many other Hawaiians shared similar experiences—instead of having things imposed from outside, something deep within was reignited. The ceremony has now become an annual event. Hawaiians are reclaiming the cultural foundation of the Aloha spirit and *ku'u'aina aloha* (my beloved homeland). They are regaining a sense of purpose, identity, foundation, and sovereignty. In this period of Ho'oulu, they are confirming an important maxim:

> It does not matter how long your spirit lies dormant and unused. One day you hear a song, look at an object, or see a vision and you feel its presence. It can't be bought, traded, or annihilated, because its power comes from its story. No one can steal your spirit. You have to give it away. You can also take it back.[193]

5. *Stories nourish spirit.*

It has been said that God created people because he loves stories. Stories by many different names play a prominent role in all the world's major religions: Christian and Sufi parables, Zen koans, the

Jewish Haggadah, Taoist allegories, the Hindu Bhagavad Gita, and Native American legends are familiar examples. Stories convey important moral lessons. Colorful, truer–than-true narratives make us laugh and move us to tears. As we listen to stories, we feel the spirit of the storyteller and are transported to places of magic and enchantment. The essence of who we are or want to be as a community seeps into our pores and fills our souls.

The late Jim Valvano, "Jimmy V," was a legendary basketball coach at North Carolina State. At the height of his career, he was diagnosed with terminal cancer. Toward the end of his battle with the disease, a tribute was convened in his honor. It was attended by hundreds, including Lou Holtz and other stalwarts of the coaching world. There was a celebratory video and heartfelt testimony from colleagues and admirers who lionized his illustrious career as a coach and the moving example his life offered to others. Then Jimmy V spoke.

He began with advice on how to live a good life. Each day, he said, spend time in reflective thought, laugh, and be moved to tears by sadness or joy. He then went on to tell a story about his early years as Rutgers University's basketball coach. He was young and wanted to make an inspirational impression on his players before the first game. He had read a book by Vince Lombardi that described the legendary coach's first pre-game pep talk to the Green Bay Packers. Lombardi barged through the doors to the locker room moments before the team was scheduled to take the field. He paced back and forth in front of his squad without speaking and then in his gravelly voice said, "Gentlemen, we will be successful this year if you keep your mind on three things, and three things only, your family, your religion, and the Green Bay Packers." The team roared onto the field and crushed their opponent.

That seemed just the ticket for Valvano—he would emulate Lombardi's strategy before Rutgers's first big game. He waited until the last minute to make his dramatic locker room entry. He tried to bang his way through the doors. They were locked—"I almost broke my arm." His assistants opened the doors and he fell on the floor.

His players were trying to help him up. Finally on his feet, he started pacing back and forth, just like Lombardi, all the while rubbing his injured arm. His eyes focused intensely on his players. He followed Lombardi's script: "Gentlemen, all eyes on me. We will be successful this year if you keep your mind on three things, and three things only, your family, your religion . . . and the Green Bay Packers." His funny story broke up the crowd, but also said a lot about the life of Jimmy V. As he told the story, you could feel his spirit and glean a valuable lesson—it's okay to make mistakes—particularly if you can laugh at yourself.[194]

Many stories are humorous and make us laugh; others are poignant and move us to tears. Schoolteachers don't make much money and, in America at least, they don't get a lot of respect. To darken the picture even more, the difference they make shows up only much later—if at all. Most often, their souls are buoyed by blind faith. Sometimes, though, they experience the magical side of their profession before they die.

Bob Deal (Terry's father, who died in 2004) retired and became deeply depressed. In reviewing his career in an inner-city elementary school, Deal wondered whether his life had taken the wrong fork in the road. He hadn't made as much money as most of his friends in other lines of work. Most of them seemed able to point to tangible results of their work. He couldn't think of any.

One evening he was bowling and the alley's cocktail waitress put a drink by his score sheet. He explained that he hadn't ordered it—he's a teetotaler. The waitress turned around and pointed, "That man ordered it for you." He stared for a few moments and then recognized him as a kid he'd taught in seventh grade twenty years before. He recognized the man because he only had one arm—the one-armed young student he had taught to play baseball despite the disability. When he and the man talked, Deal learned that the youngster had gone on to become a star baseball player in high school and college. At the end of their conversation, the man asked: "Mr. Deal, could I take you and your wife out to dinner?" They agreed on a date.

At the appointed time, a stretch limousine pulled up in front of the couple's modest home. The retiree yelled to his wife, "I think the Mafia just pulled up." A uniformed chauffer came to the door and then ushered them to the waiting limousine. As he opened the rear door, there sat the former student and his wife. The teacher and spouse were taken to a classy restaurant and then to the couple's resplendent beachfront home. The student wanted his former teacher to know how successful he had become. On the way back in the limo, the student looked closely into his teacher's eyes and said, in a voice choked with emotion, "Mr. Deal, I've waited twenty-five years to do this for you."

On hearing those few words, Mr. Deal felt that his life made sense. He knew he had made a profound difference in at least one student's life. How many more had he touched without really knowing? He didn't care. One was all he needed to restore his faith.

Stories are magic in that they create alternate realties that move us, enter us, and pull us in. We read novels, attend plays, and go to movies to escape the everyday and immerse ourselves in other lives and other worlds. Even knowing that it's only a movie or a book, we invest in the characters, feel what they feel, and worry about what will happen to them. Will the lovers find one another? Could the hero or heroine be destroyed? Will it all end happily? This power of stories to transport us to new worlds makes them a prime medium for leaders who understand the power of magic and the role of the wizard. Stories infuse life with meaning, faith, and hope:

> *Remember only this one thing,*
> *The stories people tell have a way of taking care of them.*
> *If stories come to you, care for them.*
> *And learn to give them away where they are needed.*
> *Sometimes a person needs a story more than food to stay alive.*
> *That is why we put these stories in each other's memories.*
> *This is how people care for themselves.*[195]

Summoning the human spirit does not require a complex cosmic undertaking.

Spirit is inside every living thing—most notably in people's souls. It only requires some catalyst to call it up. Following Desert Storm, five soldiers in their desert fatigues were on a flight home from Chicago to Nashville. Following standard military procedure, they were sitting in the coach cabin. To applause from their fellow travelers, a flight attendant ceremoniously moved them to first class. When the flight arrived at the gate, the soldiers were first to deplane. Down a long corridor, a crowd had assembled behind the security point. It was a sea of yellow. A five-year-old girl, with a large yellow bow in her hair, broke through security. She ran toward her fatigue-clad father and jumped in his arms. The departing passengers stopped and fell silent. Then from somewhere came the strains of a familiar melody. Without a visible leader, everyone found themselves singing "God Bless America."[196] Spirit is always there. Too often it lies dormant. Leaders who seek the wizard inside can stimulate its release.

PART SIX

THE LEADER'S JOURNEY

Fusing Warrior and Wizard

At night I relish the opportunity to indulge myself by exploring the unlimited potential of the human spirit. In the morning I don my suit of armor and head off to battle the dark forces at work. I am struggling to integrate the two roles.

—PAUL HOUSTON

Houston, who heads up the American Association of School Administrators, knows that good leaders balance the political and spiritual aspects of their roles. He writes about it in hopes of firing the imaginations of those who lead schools and educate children. He recognizes that the greatest leaders, those who have had the most profound impact on their organization or their times, have found ways to emulate both warrior and wizard. They blend the two images or move fluidly between the two as circumstances demand. In the final chapters, we try to fill a major void in the way leaders think about leadership and make it happen.

Though the potentials for wizard and warrior coexist in all of us, our gifts differ, and some of us are more determined than others to develop and use the gifts we have. In every walk of life and historical era, we find individuals who have exemplified the characteristics of both authentic wizard and principled warrior. Each is unique and inspirational, and each offers a story that has much to teach about leadership at its best.

These stories reflect universal elements that compose a shared script for the drama of leadership. The common story-line begins with a group (or organization or society) that has lost its way or is falling apart. Sometimes the group is complacent and in denial. In other cases, it is dispirited and discouraged. In any event, people resign themselves to existing realities and find it hard to imagine that things could ever improve. Then a new leader appears, often from outside the group, to inspire a glimmer of hope and to point the way to a more promising future.

Leaders who rise to such an occasion meld the core capacities of wizard and warrior into a unique approach. These intertwined qualities include courage, faith, creativity, and passion. Courage enables the leader to persist in the face of dangers and personal costs. Passion supports a level of aspiration that goes well beyond what others see as realistic. Faith derives from a profound conviction that the chosen purpose is both worthy and achievable. Creativity offers challenging and inspiring new ways to frame where we are and where we can go from here. The combination of these qualities produces magic—the impossible becomes possible, and the once deflated and dispirited group or organization looks and feels different.

In the chapters to come we focus on the intersection of wizard and warrior ways. Chapter Fifteen examines two ancient Japanese images—the ninja and the samurai. Each suggests a different way of balancing the skills and orientations of wizard and warrior. The next four chapters are devoted to leaders whose stories highlight efforts to combine wizardly and warrior-like qualities. We will spotlight important lessons along the way, but much of the learning is embedded in the narratives themselves.

Chapter Sixteen follows an emblematic American corporation, IBM, through nine decades, focusing on two larger-than-life chief executives who made a difference at historic crossroads—first to make IBM great and later to return it to greatness. Chapter Seventeen leaps back six centuries to medieval France and the extraordinary story of Joan of Arc, who teaches us that deep faith is the wellspring of uncommon courage. Chapter Eighteen fast-forwards to the late 1900s, where we meet Tex Gunning, an executive who combined creativity with dogged persistence to engineer a remarkable transformation of a Dutch food company. Chapter Nineteen examines the career of the great civil rights leader, Martin Luther King Jr., whose passion sustained the struggle to achieve a dream of justice and freedom for all Americans.

Chapter Twenty outlines steps you can take to develop your capabilities as both wizard and warrior. We close with Chapter Twenty-One, "The Sword and the Wand," which summarizes the book's key lessons about infusing power and passion into contemporary organizations.

15

PERSONAL JOURNEY

The Ninja and the Samurai

The wizard relies more heavily on magic and mystery, the warrior on strength and skill. These two distinct ways were personified in ancient Japan by the ninja, who relied on subtlety and artfulness, and the samurai, who emphasized power and physical prowess. But there was also strength in the ninja and some magic in the samurai. Both were bred for a world that has parallels today in the contrast between conventional soldiers and special forces or guerillas. Ninja and samurai have become archetypes, known around the world in story, myth, and film, because each represents a distinctive resolution of the tension between wizard and warrior.

The samurai was a rough analogue of medieval Europe's knight—an armored, aristocratic warrior, famed for martial prowess and adherence to a demanding code of conduct. Beginning around the tenth century, the samurai evolved as a professional warrior class who played an expanding social and political role. Samurai served as administrators, police officers, and provincial officials.[197] An era of weak central authority and chronic civil war propelled the samurai up the social ladder, giving them a powerful role in Japanese culture and politics.

In the samurai ideal, loyalty to one's master and a Zen-like detachment from fear of death were among the highest virtues. Like the knight, the samurai fought openly and directly, favoring worthy opponents. Real samurai, being human, often fell short of the ideal, but at best the samurai provided a highly respected model of courage and strength.[198]

The ninja emerged in the same historical era, but had different origins, mastered different skills, and played by different rules. Where the samurai were aristocrats, the ninja were commoners. The samurai sought honor and prestige in open combat; the ninja had no reputation or name to protect, and they preferred to remain behind the scenes.[199] The samurai fought face-to-face. The ninja used stealth and craftiness, avoiding direct combat whenever possible. The samurai was a swordsman. Ninjas were snoops, snipers, subversives, and magicians. At their best, they achieved their ends as if by magic. Ninjas were famous for their invisibility—their ability to destroy enemy morale or eliminate the enemy's commander without anyone's knowing how or by whose hand it came about.

The samurai was often contemptuous of the ninja. His skills and weapons gave him a great advantage in direct combat, but such a battle offered little to either party. There was small glory for the samurai in defeating so unworthy an opponent. For the ninja, head-on combat represented failure, not success. The ninja's advantage was that he was not bound by the samurai's code of conduct. To the samurai, the ninja's unconventional techniques and behind-the-back operations were shameful and cowardly. The ninja was less fastidious about method—all was fair in war if it achieved the valued objective. This made the ninja very valuable to any feuding warlord who hoped to save blood and treasure by surreptitiously bumping off his counterparts.

Ninja and samurai live on as exemplars of two paths, with distinctive strategies and skill sets. The samurai represents the way of open combat for warriors who rely on courage, strength, and skill to achieve victory. The ninja way involves cunning, illusion, secrecy, and stealth. These paths are not mutually exclusive, and many leaders will use a mix of the two shaped by their skills, weapons at hand, and immediate circumstances. Neither way is necessarily more praiseworthy or ethical. At first glance, the ninja way of stealth and illusion may seem less admirable than the open courage of the samurai. But in war, deception is often critical for saving lives as well as winning battles. Sun Tzu wrote that deception is central to warfare,[200] and legendary Civil War General Stonewall Jackson's rule number 1 was "Mystify, mislead and surprise."[201]

In World War II, the Allies' greatest advantage in planning for D-Day was that they knew where they would attack, and the Germans did not. The Allies mounted an elaborate scheme to convince the Germans that the invasion would begin with a British attack on Norway, followed by an American invasion at Pas de Calais, France. The primary force was to be under the command of General George Patton. "The notion of Patton's personal involvement was crucial in the deception, for the Germans had a high regard for his abilities and assumed he would lead the main effort. His imaginary army had dummy troops, make-believe exercises, and contrived radio traffic conducted with deliberate indiscretion."[202] The ruse was so effective that weeks after D-Day, the Germans still maintained an army at Pas de Calais waiting for Patton's attack.[203]

Leaders continually confront a series of choices between the ways of the samurai and those of the ninja—between directness and indirection, openness and stealth, reality and illusion, force and subtlety. Several questions can help them choose one course or another.

1. *Am I strong or weak?*

When strong, be a samurai. When you have a larger army, more market power, or more friends and allies than your competitors, open combat works to your advantage. When weak, be a ninja. When your competitors hold a stronger hand, a frontal attack may be suicidal. You need the sort of thing Mao Zedong explains here:

> In guerrilla warfare, select the tactic of seeming to come from the east and attacking from the west; avoid the solid, attack the hollow; attack; withdraw; deliver a lightning blow, seek a lightning decision. When guerrillas engage a stronger enemy, they withdraw when he advances; harass him when he stops; strike him when he is weary; pursue him when he withdraws. In guerilla strategy, the enemy's rear, flanks, and other vulnerable spots are his vital points, and there he must be harassed, attacked, dispersed, exhausted and annihilated.[204]

Clausewitz argued that the more desperate your position, the more likely that your best option is a long-odds roll of the dice: "But the weaker the forces become which are under the command of strategy, so much the more they become adapted for stratagem, so that to the quite feeble and little, for whom no prudence, no sagacity is any longer sufficient at the point where all art seems to forsake him, stratagem offers itself as a last resource."[205]

2. *What are the rules of the game?*

In organized sports, the rules are codified and enforced by umpires or referees. Elsewhere, rules are usually fuzzier and enforcement is often lax or nonexistent: "All's fair in love and war." Leaders must determine which doctrine they need to follow and what they safely can ignore. They must be willing at times to violate conventional wisdom and rules in the service of a larger cause, but still anticipate the risks. Many entrepreneurs who built great businesses have run afoul of the law. Entrepreneurs like Bill Gates (Microsoft) and Sam Walton (Wal-Mart) destroyed as they created. They put many smaller, weaker firms out of business. The result was that they made enemies and sometimes ran into legal trouble. Early in his career, Tom Watson, the founder of IBM, was prosecuted for a criminal conspiracy to restrain trade; he was convicted, fined $5,000, and sentenced to a year in jail. The jail sentence was ultimately suspended, but Watson never lost his distaste for the American legal system.

Karl Rove, widely viewed as the political architect of the George W. Bush presidency, is admired by his allies for his political brilliance—and despised by opponents who view him as a master of deceit and dirty tricks. His critics note that, over the years, opponents of Rove's candidates suffered a remarkable run of bad luck. At key moments in a campaign, they were suddenly put on the defensive by a damaging rumor, a leaked investigation, or a savage attack by a mysterious new group that materialized from thin air (usually with financial support from a wealthy Texas Republican). The same script repeated itself in one campaign after another. The opponents always cried foul, and Rove's candidate always said that he (rarely she) was running a positive campaign on the issues and had no connection to whatever misfortune had befallen his opponent. An early example occurred in a gubernatorial campaign in Texas. On the eve of the first televised debate, an electronic bug was found in Rove's office by a security firm he hired. Rove immediately called police and reporters to report this surprising discovery. He didn't say, but did imply, that this was the work of his Democratic opponents. Every newspaper and television station in Texas carried the story, and the Democrat found himself on the defensive, trying to convince people he knew nothing about it. Investigators eventually concluded that Rove might have arranged for the bug himself, but by then the campaign was over and Rove's man had won.[206] Variations on this scenario repeated themselves in one election after another, right up to the time that a new organization, "Swift Boat Veterans for Truth," emerged during the 2004 presidential campaign suggesting that Bush's opponent, John Kerry, was no war hero.

Pushing the boundaries is part of leadership, but the harder you push, the more you need good judgment about how far is too far. At what point do the costs outweigh the gains because you goad your enemies into action, alienate your allies, or face damaging legal consequences? Leaders' supporters will usually tolerate stretching the rules up to a point, but may fall away if leaders go too far. Many of President Bill Clinton's supporters were reluctant to judge him too harshly in the face of the sex-and-cover-up scandal that nearly brought down his presidency. But he and his intended successor, Al Gore, paid a high price. The scandal, compounded by Gore's decision to distance himself from his damaged benefactor, very likely cost Gore the presidency in the breathtakingly close election of 2000.

Leaders must also understand that not everyone has to play by the same rules. Historically, the ninja had the advantage of flexibility in a battle with a samurai, who was bound by rules the ninja could ignore. Gandhi used a similar principle in battling British rule in India, which was codified by Saul Alinsky in his *Rules for Radicals:* Insist that the powerful follow their own rules, while your side works from its own less-restrictive playbook.[207]

3. *What do my values tell me?*

They're your values. Always give them top priority. Your leadership will be rudderless if you don't know (or ignore) what is most dear to you. Don't get caught up in a long list of motherhood and Boy Scout ideals, but spotlight what you deeply and genuinely care about, particularly in the long term. Leaders make their worst mistakes responding to powerful short-term pressures and ignoring soulful messages from their spiritual core.

In the late 1990s, Kenneth Lay and Jeffrey Skilling committed themselves to getting Enron recognized as "The World's Greatest Company." They might have succeeded had they not been so obsessed with the stock price and short-term earnings growth. Knowingly or not, they created a climate that enabled their chief financial officer, Andrew Fastow, to embark on murky or illegal financial manipulations that eventually destroyed the company. Wise leaders know that they must sometimes sacrifice in the short term to achieve a greater victory down the road. Those who insist on winning every battle may never win the long-term war.

The ninja and the samurai each embodies a distinct leadership approach. The samurai is an exemplar of the heroic warrior who wins through strength, valor, and skill in open combat. The ninja, conversely, is a shadowy magician, a secret agent or clandestine assailant who avoids direct combat and relies instead on strategy, illusion, secrecy, and magic to achieve victory. The choice of one path or the other depends on your assets and circumstances. It is often advantageous to be a samurai when your position is strong, but a ninja when you are weak. But you also need to take into account your own values and the existing rules of the game. Rule-breaking is sometimes the only way to win, but leaders always need to be mindful of the associated risks. Warriors adhere to a prevailing code of ethics; wizards rely on mystery and magic to circumvent prevailing doctrine.

16

LEARNING TO LEAD

The Genesis and Rebirth of IBM

In his early years, Thomas J. Watson showed little evidence of great talent or leadership potential, but he had one great asset—a tremendous desire to learn. Like a highly motivated toddler, Watson tried things, fell, got back on his feet, and tried again, always gleaning lessons from his missteps. He mined his experience, studied exemplars, and sought tutelage wherever he could. It paid off later in his career when the knowledge and wisdom he had acquired enabled him to turn an obscure and struggling company into one of the world's greatest—IBM. The pupil became a teacher.

*W*atson launched his career by failing—first as a school-teacher, and then as co-owner of a butcher shop in Buffalo. The second setback had a serendipitous silver lining. Watson's partner had made off with the cash, but not the cash register. Watson went to return the register to the local office of National Cash Register (NCR), and wound up going to work for "the Cash" as a salesman in 1896. Initially, he wasn't very good at selling either, and complained to his boss, John Range, that no one wanted to buy a cash register. The interchange is instructive: "'Of course not,' Range replied. If they *wanted* to buy them they'd come into the office and get them themselves, and the company would be spared the trouble and expense of supporting sad excuses for sales-men like you.' What Watson had to find out was *why* they didn't. Then he'd be half way to changing their minds. Watson listened and learned."[208] He shadowed Range on calls, soaked up everything he could, and soon became one of the best salesmen in the company.

Success brought him to the attention of John Patterson, the crusty autocrat who ran NCR. This turned out to be a mixed blessing since Patterson's flaws were almost as majestic as his many talents. Patterson offered Watson an assignment so special that the Cash would deny any connection to it. He set up Watson with his own independent business—Watson's Cash Register and Second Hand Exchange—in New York City. Its purpose wasn't to make money but to drive NCR's competitors out of business. "Watson's New York company engaged in tactics that started as razor-sharp and ended as fraudulent. Watson and his subordinates engaged in commercial espionage, spying on rivals and their rivals' customers. They set up shop next door to com-petitors and practiced predatory pricing unconstrained by any profit considerations."[209]

Most egregious were the "knockoff machines" that carried the look and brand of competitors' products. Watson's company sold them for half the price of the genuine article, and then let the com-petitor take the rap when the machines broke down, as they did often. This scheme worked so well that Patterson moved Watson first to Philadelphia and later to Chicago to work the same dirty tricks. These shenanigans eventually caught the attention of the U.S. Attorney General. Watson and Patterson were indicted, convicted, and sentenced to a year in jail. They escaped only because of the great Dayton flood of 1913—an event eerily similar to the flood in New Orleans in 2005. Levees broke, and downtown Dayton was under more than twelve feet of water. NCR, situated on high ground, turned its headquarters into a refugee center for more than two thousand people—much like the Superdome in the aftermath of Hurricane Katrina. Patterson and Watson's tireless efforts on flood relief made them local heroes and got them off the legal hook.

In 1914 Patterson, following an old habit with star subordinates, fired Watson. It turned out to be a favor. Watson had learned much from Patterson, and his track record made him a hot prospect in the executive search world of the time. He was brought in to run an emerging but beleaguered company, Computing Tabulating and Recording (CTR). Some of CTR's board members were skeptical because of Watson's earlier conviction. "Who's going to run the business while he serves his time in jail?" growled one director.[210] Watson was not a technical whiz and knew little about CTR's products. But he took the lessons he learned at NCR, added some ideas developed on his own, and cobbled up an approach to running the company. It included an unofficial dress code favoring a formal appearance; a headquarters that set a standard of elegance for the industry; a binding no-drinking norm; a set of values, including integrity, honor, decency, formality, and politeness; an annual awards event—the Hundred Percent Club—plus an employee country club and training facility and a company-wide newsletter. These would lay the cultural foundation for International Business Machines (IBM).

Most of these patterns and practices were not edicts. They were infused by Watson's behavior and his optimistic outlook for the future of the company. His pep talks at sales meeting were legendary.

A typical example: "You have to put your heart in the business and the business in your heart. A team that can't be beat won't be beat."[211] The message was reinforced as the salesmen sang songs in honor of the boss:

> *Mr. Watson is the man we're working for;*
>
> *He's the leader of the CTR.*
>
> *He's the fairest, squarest man we know.*
>
> *Sincere and true, he has shown us how to play the game*
>
> *And how to make the dough.*[212]

Watson delivered the dough. Sales doubled in his first three years. In 1924 he renamed the company International Business Machines, refocused the product line on machines that processed information, and emphasized that IBM was really selling service. During the 1930s, a bad time for American business, Watson embraced the New Deal, won a contract to supply machines for the new Social Security Administration, and managed to double IBM's revenues.

For more than half a century, IBM set the standard for American business, and its sterling reputation spread worldwide. When Peter Drucker quizzed a group of Japanese about Japan's remarkable post-war business success, the response caught him off guard: "'Don't you realize,' my Japanese friends asked, 'that we are simply adapting what IBM has done all along?' And when I ask how come, they always say, 'When we started to rebuild Japan in the 1950s, we looked around for the most successful company we could find. It's IBM, isn't it?'"[213]

Most of the key ingredients of IBM's success could be traced directly to Thomas J. Watson. His personality and ideas shaped the company from the early punch-card machines to IBM's entry into the electronic age. His intuition was usually on target, though some-times he also needed a large measure of luck. To the point of dicta-torship, he demanded excellence in everything employees took on. But a softer side encouraged the IBM songs and frivolity that graced every special event. As business sage Peter Drucker observed: "It's hard to describe the warmth of the man. He could turn it on. It was an art. But if there had been a *Harvard Business Review* [in the 1930s], it would have run stories about him, and he would have been considered a nut or a crank."[214] Watson's attention to the symbols of IBM reflected an understanding of the importance of corporate culture long before the term was invented. That culture wove IBM's employees together in a common quest and bested the competition time and again.

IBM's culture was unified around one word—THINK. It was posted everywhere and became a well-known symbol both inside and outside the company. But there was more to the social fabric that captured the hearts and souls of employees and compensated for Watson's inadequacies as a manager. People did things the IBM way without being told because they knew what was valued. A simple statement of Basic Beliefs laid it out:

- Excellence in every thing we do.

- Superior customer service.

- Respect for the individual.

These were more than platitudes on a plaque or hyperbole in speeches. They were stitched into people's hearts and souls and served as guides for everyday behavior.

Other practices and events reinforced the values and beliefs and created a company-wide sense of cohesion and passion: The lavish celebration and recognition of the Hundred Percent Club. IBM Day at the World's Fair. The IBM Country Club open to IBM employees and their families. A monthly magazine—*THINK*. The Homestead, a large old country lodge with its camplike atmosphere and Spartan living quarters, where executives, employees, and customers could mingle in a relaxed atmosphere. All these created and reinforced the symbolic glue that made IBM a powerhouse of American business. "Success

didn't come from the culture alone, however. It needed a magic ingredient that would light up the culture and turn IBM into a business
rocket—a pinch of something that would make all the difference in
the world. That ingredient was Watson's daring."[215] It was a magical
time and Thomas Watson Sr. was the wizard who waved the wand,
creating the enchantment and excitement.

In the early 1950s, Thomas Watson Jr. inherited the magic cloak
from his father. He kept the keys to the cultural treasures that had
guided IBM through tough times before. But he also turned the company in another direction—the age of electronics. When Remington
Rand's UNIVAC computer posed a formidable threat to IBM's dom-
inance of the industry, IBM responded with innovative lines of electronic computers. The company's products were not necessarily
technically superior to the competition, but IBM's legendary commitment to service enabled it to trump the competition. And through
Watson Jr.'s inspired leadership, coupled with IBM's cultural heritage,
the company achieved record levels of growth and profitability.

Thomas Watson Jr. stepped down from the IBM board in 1985,
and in the years that followed, IBM began to stumble. It misread
the Watson legacy, focusing more on time-worn precepts than on the
learning that had produced them. Its cultural values drifted and ossified around lessons from the past. Striving for excellence too often
turned into an obsessive perfectionism that slowed the development
of new products. IBM lost its competitive edge, allowing itself to fall
behind in minicomputers in the 1970s and personal computers a
decade later. Superior customer service deteriorated to pushing what
the company wanted to sell, rather than figuring out what customers
needed. Respect for the individual was distorted into letting people
do whatever they wanted. Individual fiefdoms undercut a firmwide
focus and spawned costly duplication. Even the "dark suit, white
shirt" practice lost its appeal to customers in an environment of more
casual business dress. IBMers stuck out like old-fashioned sore thumbs.
Outside analysts advocated breaking the company up. IBM's internal

focus and arrogance prevented a search for better solutions. Worst of all, Tom Watson's creation lost its sense of magic and passion.

Lou Gerstner Jr. was chosen by IBM's board to restore the company to its lost level of performance and profitability. Onlookers both inside and outside assumed that Gerstner would bring to IBM what he was known for in his two preceding positions as CEO—at RJR Nabisco and American Express: strategy, analysis, and measurement. He seemed to confirm this expectation during his first meeting with the press. When asked about his vision for the company, he responded, "The last thing IBM needs is a vision." But Gerstner had no intention of simply repeating a leadership script learned in his prior jobs. He was as committed to learning as Thomas J. Watson had been. He paid close attention to IBM's language, believing you can learn a lot by listening to how a company talks. He noted that IBM had its own vocabulary, with terms like "down-level" and "LOBs" that made sense only to the initiated.[216] To Gerstner it was evidence of how insular IBM had become. Gerstner also asked lots of questions:

> I asked one of the most senior executives to provide me with a detailed analysis of a major money-losing business at IBM. I did this not only because I wanted the insight but also to test this highly-rated executive. Three days later, I asked him how the work was progressing. He said, "I'll check with the team and get back to you." At the end of the week I got the same response. When this little scene played out a third time, I finally said, "Why don't you just give me the name of the person doing the work, and from now on I'll speak directly with him or her." What I discovered was that senior executives often presided. They organized work and then waited to review it when it was done.[217]

As he learned more, Gerstner found much that needed changing in IBM's practices, but he became a growing admirer of IBM's values.

He realized that his primary challenge would be to revitalize a culture that had lost its way:

> In the end, my deepest culture-change goal was to induce IBMers to believe in themselves again—to believe that they had the ability to determine their own fate, and that they *already* knew what they needed to know. It was to shake them out of their depressed stupor, remind them of who they were—you're *IBM,* damn it!—and get them to think and act collaboratively, as hungry, curious self-starters.[218]

In the beginning, Gerstner laid out a strategy: keep the company together, reinvest in the tired mainframe business, stick with the core semiconductor business, protect the historical commitment to R&D, focus on the customer rather than internal issues, and become more market-driven.[219] But over time Gerstner shifted his perspective:

> I came to see in my time at IBM, that culture isn't just one aspect of the game—it *is* the game. In the end an organization is nothing more than the collective capacity of its people to create value. Vision, strategy, marketing, financial management—any management system, in fact—can set you on the right path and can carry you for a while. But no enterprise—whether in business, government, education, health care, or *any* area of human endeavor—will succeed over the long haul if those elements aren't part of its DNA.[220]

Gerstner was successful in rallying the troops and saving IBM. As he passed the torch to his successor, the company had once again become a robust and widely admired institution. Gerstner's final letter to executives, managers, and employees encapsulates the spirit of the turnaround:

With the support and leadership of thousands of IBMers, we did turn the company around. That work, and my initial mandate, was largely completed by the mid-nineties. But along the way, something happened—something that, quite frankly, surprised me. I fell in love with IBM. I decided, like many of you, that this was the best company in the world."[221]

IBM became great, and was later restored to greatness, by leaders whose instincts for learning helped them combine the warrior's tenacity and competitive instinct with the magic of wizards of yore. Thomas Watson Sr. and Lou Gerstner Jr. were competitive to their core, but they both relied heavily on symbols to work their magic. Watson as the creator of IBM harkens us back to Merlin, Gandalf, and Dumbledore. All dispensed advice without insisting that it be followed. Their ability to predict the future was not flawless, but their guesses were usually right on target.

Lou Gerstner said of himself that he "hates, hates, hates to lose."[222] When he was first approached for IBM's top job, Gerstner said no because he feared it was a losing proposition—his lack of a technical background, combined with IBM's deep troubles, might put him on a field where he could not win. Once he took the job, he attacked many of IBM's old ways and failing products with a vengeance. Layoffs, firings, and decapitations of sacred cows were all part of the initial shakeup. Yet in Gerstner's transformation of IBM, we also see a deep sensitivity to the cultural roots of the company and ability to separate core beliefs from peripheral, often outmoded, prac- tices. His emphasis on helping IBMers believe in themselves again and on having the faith to restore the company to its former pinnacle of performance is very similar to the strategy of another well-known wizard—the Wizard of Oz. When the Great Oz was exposed as merely a man, his advice to Dorothy and her companions on the yellow brick road was profound. What they were searching for was inside. As a contemporary CEO once observed: "My primary job is selling hot hope." Many of today's ossified organizations need an infusion of hope, passion, faith, belief, and meaning. They also need fearless warriors like Watson and Gerstner who will let nothing stand in the way of victory. The combination of the two produces extraordinary results.

17

LEADING WITH COURAGE AND FAITH

Joan of Arc

It takes courage and faith to set the pace because showing the way is inherently dangerous. Leaders must encourage constituents to undertake hazardous journeys that carry no guarantee of a happy ending. Those who lead are regularly attacked by their enemies and often rejected by their friends. Without courage leaders can provide only timid and ineffectual leadership. Leaders also need faith. They must believe that their cause is worthy and achievable, regardless of hardships and setbacks along the way.

Courage is a hallmark of warriors, and faith is essential to wizards. But these two qualities intermingle. Courage sustains faith under fire, and faith provides a purpose for being courageous. Few have demonstrated the interplay between faith and courage more vividly than Joan of Arc, the warrior saint.

LA PUCELLE ("THE MAID")

In her time, she was known simply as the Maid (*La Pucelle* in French). Since then, she has been the heroine of more than twenty feature films and hundreds of poems, plays, operas, and symphonies. She was declared a saint by the Catholic Church in 1920, and her feast day is a national holiday in France. She earned all that fame and honor in an astonishingly brief period—"one year of combat, and one year of prison"—She was only nineteen when burned alive in 1431.[223] Courage rooted in unshakeable faith was essential to the miraculous achievements of the visionary, soldier, and martyr known as Joan of Arc.

She was born in 1412 to a peasant family in the small French village of Domrémy. Her parents were "laborers, good and true Catholics, honest folk and worthy, according to their ability, but not rich."[224] France at the time was divided and dispirited: "turned upside down, a footstool for mankind, the winepress of the English, a boot-wipe for brigands."[225] It had suffered and splintered through eighty years of the Hundred Years War as various English and French claimants fought for control. In Joan's time, the war was a complicated, three-way competition among the dauphin (Crown Prince Charles), the king of England (Henry VI), and the duke of Burgundy (Philip the Good). Their squabbles embodied larger issues of identity and independence: Would France be ruled by the oft-despised English, or would it control its own destiny?

Domrémy was in a frontier region under English sway, but the village itself was loyal to the dauphin. Her neighbors remembered young Joan as, in many ways, a girl "just like everyone else."[226] She did typical women's work like spinning and housework, and she helped her father in the fields. She was distinctive in two ways: her commitment to the Catholic faith was unusually deep, even for a pious age, and she did everything with unusual enthusiasm. "Willingly" was the word her neighbors used more than any other to capture her character.

In her thirteenth year, she first heard God's voice calling her. She was frightened, but the message was reassuring—she should conduct herself well, and go to church.[227] As time passed, she heard multiple voices. The messages evolved and became both amazing and alarming. They told her that it was her mission to go to the aid of the dauphin and lead him to the ancient city of Reims, where he could finally be crowned as the legitimate king of France. Joan protested that she was only a poor girl who was hardly suited for such a mission. But the voices persisted and eventually became very specific. She was to go to a nearby fortress city and enlist the aid of the captain there. He would give her companions to go with her to the court.[228]

FAITH IS THE WELLSPRING OF COURAGE

Heeding this call was truly a heroic act for Joan. The message she was to deliver could not have been more incredible: "She had come from her Lord so that he would tell the Dauphin to stand fast and not make war on his enemies, for the Lord would bring him help before the next mid-Lent."[229] She could not have found the courage to do this without great faith both in herself and in her call from God.

What followed was one of history's more remarkable stories. Joan arrived at the court in Chinon near the end of February 1429, when she was barely seventeen. Skeptical but curious, the dauphin sent retainers to ask who she was and what she wanted. Her answer strained credibility: she had a mandate from God first to raise the siege of Orléans, then to lead Charles to Reims to be crowned. She added, "He will have no help if not through me."[230] The interrogators returned from their mission divided. Some believed the girl was mad and should be sent away immediately. Others, impressed by Joan's piety and confidence, felt that the dauphin should see her.

Joan came before the court the following evening. It must have been an extraordinary experience for her. A witness reported:

> Then Joan, having come before the king, made the curtsies and reverences that customarily are made to a king as though she had been nourished at the court, and her greeting having been delivered, said in addressing the king, "God give you life, gentle King," even though she did not know him and had never seen him, and there were many pompous lords there more opulently dressed than was the king. Wherefore he replied to Joan: "What if I am not the king, Joan?" Pointing to one of the lords, he said: "There is the king." To which she answered, "In God's name gentle Prince, it is you and none other."[231]

The king began to question her, and she told him, "I say to you, on behalf of the Lord, that you are the true heir of France, and a king's son, and He has sent me to you to lead you to Reims, so that you can receive your coronation and consecration if you wish it."[232]

As skeptical as Charles was about help from such an unexpected quarter, the temptation to believe this remarkable young woman would have been very strong. Joan was an extraordinary presence— wise beyond her years, articulate, energetic, and possessed of a deep faith that made her utterly confident in her vision. Her message— that she was sent from God to establish that he was the true heir and "a king's son"—was certainly one that Charles wanted to hear.

On his father's death in 1422, supported by powerful French noble families, Charles declared himself the heir to the throne. Subsequently, his efforts to sustain that claim had gone badly. The English dismissively referred to him as the "King of Bourges" because he controlled only a relatively small part of the south of France. Charles needed a gift from heaven, and Joan promised just that. A cautious man, Charles still took the additional precaution of having Joan examined by a group of learned clergy and professors. They were duly impressed, one commenting, "She spoke terribly well. I would really like to have had so fine a daughter."[233] Asked, for example, why soldiers were even needed if God wanted to liberate France, she answered, "In God's name, the soldiers will give battle and God will give the victory."[234]

The king now decided to provide Joan with armor, horses, and an army to go with her to Orléans. The city had been under siege by a large English force for about six months, and "on the fate of Orléans hung that of the entire Kingdom."[235] The English were gradually tightening the noose around the city, and all but one route in and out had been closed off. A French effort to relieve the city had ended in disaster only a few weeks before Joan's arrival at the court. The citizens of Orléans were in despair, and the fall of the city seemed imminent.

Joan's arrival at Orléans was much anticipated, and she was greeted by a large crowd eager to see and touch her. Her first combat came on Wednesday, May 4, five days after she arrived. One chronicler reported, "The English were preparing themselves for battle when Joan suddenly arrived before them. As soon as the French saw Joan they began to raise a shout and took the bastille of Saint-Loup."[236] It was only a skirmish, but her first combat foray was a success.

Friday and Saturday were decisive. The military commanders had less faith than Joan did, and tried to dissuade her from making an attack, but she went out anyway. By now, her army believed in her. They won major victories on Friday, and succeeded in liberating the city a day later. The English left swiftly, leaving behind much of their supplies and equipment. In less than a week, Joan had fulfilled the first of her promises. The siege of Orléans had been lifted. Her faith had made all the difference. Soldiers who had expected to lose suddenly expected to win because the Maid had promised that God was on their side. This gave them the courage and determination to make the promise come true.

Joan returned almost immediately to the dauphin to urge him to prepare for the journey to Reims for his coronation. Living in a world that was far more political than spiritual, Charles and many of his counselors debated and delayed. It was a daunting initiative that would require journeying deep into hostile territory. But Joan was confident and convincing, and Charles finally assented to the effort. Joan rode at the head of a large royal army that set out to dislodge enemy forces and open the route to Reims. On June 17, the French encountered a formidable English force on a plain near a small country town. Seeing the English, Joan called out to her army, "God sends them to us for punishment! Today the gentle king will have his greatest victory ever!"[237] Her prediction was dead-on—the battle was a catastrophe for the English. The road to Reims lay wide open.

On July 17, 1429, less than five months after Joan had come on the scene, the dauphin was crowned at Reims as Charles VII, following a tradition almost a thousand years old. After clergy and nobles had paid homage to the new king, Joan knelt before him, embraced his legs and said: "Gentle king, from this moment the pleasure of God is executed. He wished me to raise the siege of Orléans and bring you to the city of Reims to receive your anointing, which shows that you are the true king and the one to whom the kingdom should belong."[238]

Joan's fame spread throughout France and beyond. The nation was aroused and Joan was eager to ride the tide of enthusiasm forward in a campaign to drive the English out of France. Charles and many of his advisers preferred delay and diplomacy to battle. The Maid had done what Charles needed and he habitually became jealous of any in his retinue who might eclipse his glory. Now that he was king and free of the shadow of illegitimacy, he became less willing to follow Joan's counsel. He seemed to feel that Joan was becoming a nag. To get her out of the way, he assigned her to go after bandits in another part of the realm.

In April 1430, Joan heard from her voices that she would be taken prisoner. That prediction soon came true. She was captured by forces of the duke of Burgundy, and sold to the English for the extraordinary sum of ten thousand pounds. On Christmas Eve, 1430, she was delivered to Rouen for an ecclesiastical trial. The remarkable thing about the trial was not the result—a guilty verdict was foreordained—but how difficult it was to achieve. Much of the trial was spent in a largely fruitless search for a credible hook on which to hang a verdict of heresy. An inquiry in her homeland failed to turn up anything helpful to the prosecution. After interviewing numerous witnesses in her hometown, the prosecutor's representative reported that he "had found nothing about Joan that he would not wish to find about his own sister."[239]

It should have been an easy victory for the prosecution. Joan was utterly alone, a barely literate country girl. She had no counsel and was deprived of contact with anyone who could be counted as a friend or ally. Her judges included a panoply of eminent clergy, including bishops, professors, and the rector of the university of Paris. Despite those odds, Joan held her own over the five months of the trial. She was articulate, combative, often witty, and sometimes insolent.

Her speech was often eloquent. When she was asked, "Do you know if you are in the grace of God now?" she replied, "If I am not, may God put me there. And if I am, may God keep me there, for I would be the most sorrowful woman in the world if I knew that I was not in the grace of God." A witness declared that "Those who were interrogating her were stupefied."[240]

Both the interrogators and Joan herself returned often to the topic of her voices. The court tried to extract testimony to support a charge of sorcery, but she was vigorous in her denials. Joan consistently indicated that her "voices had nothing to say about the judges' preoccupation with mandrakes, good-luck rings, or popular magic formulae."[241]

For much of the trial, Joan held to the belief that God would somehow deliver her from her captors, but as time went on, she began to see that her delivery might come only through death. "My voices say, 'take everything serenely, do not shrink from your martyrdom; from that you will come finally to the kingdom of paradise.'"[242]

Throughout the ordeal, she steadily maintained her faith in her voices, indicating that "she feared above all to exceed what her voices had dictated, to be an insufficiently faithful instrument."[243] In Joan's words, "I have greater fear of failing my voices in saying something that displeases them than I have of answering you."[244]

A verdict was finally issued at the end of May, in 1431. On May 31, Joan was delivered to the secular authorities to be burned in the public market of Rouen. Tied to the stake, she continued to call out in praise of God and the saints. She asked for a cross, and an Englishman made her a small one from a stick and handed it to her. "She took it devoutly and kissed it, making a pious lamentation to God, our redeemer, who had suffered on the cross, of which cross she had the sign and representation, and she put that cross in her bosom, between her flesh and her garments. Her last word, in a high voice, was, 'Jesus.'"[245]

Later the same day, the executioner told a priest that he felt damned because he had burned a holy woman.[246] Twenty-five years after her death, Joan was exonerated, and her original trial was declared null and void. In 1920, she was canonized as a saint of the Roman Catholic Church.

ORIGINS OF FAITH

Whether Joan's voices came from God or from within herself, they were at the core of her power and impact. What mattered was that *she* believed them, and so did many of her followers. Her voices provided her with an unshakeable faith that gave her the courage to lead. Her faith also inspired a vision that reframed the political and military reality of France. Nothing about that reality changed with her entry on the scene, and yet, magically, everything was different. The story she told inspired her allies and frightened her opponents.

Joan was the new leader who entered a dispirited land, bringing creativity, passion, faith, and courage. Charles and his followers were descending into gloom, but Joan brought wonderful news—God would bring victory. Her courage, expressed in her repeated willingness to put her life on the line, gave proof of her conviction. Her passion for her mission and confidence that it would be accomplished moved almost all who heard her. She changed history as a result.

18

CREATIVE CONFRONTATION

Willem "Tex" Gunning

Thomas J. Watson and Lou Gerstner developed as leaders by aggressively exploiting opportunities to learn. Joan of Arc's faith gave her the courage to lead and accomplish seemingly impossible feats. Fast-forward to Holland in the late twentieth century. We meet a leader who confirms these lessons while exemplifying another quality of great leaders—the ability to combine creativity with confrontation. "Tough bastard" and "poet and preacher" have both been used to describe Willem "Tex" Gunning, a Dutch business executive with a record of leading remarkable business transformations. Part of his story is told in a fascinating book, *To the Desert and Back,* by Philip Mirvis, Karen Ayas, and George Roth.[247] Growing up in Holland, Tex Gunning was a rebellious free spirit with a flair for the dramatic. The son of a Dutch marine killed in the Korean War, Gunning enlisted early—but his military career was brief and unheroic. It ended prematurely after he showed up one evening for a formal "dress blues" occasion wearing blue jeans. "'I learned an enormous lesson from this,' he remembered. 'I didn't accomplish anything by just fighting against the system. I would have to do things differently in corporate life.'"[248]

Still youthful but wiser, Gunning joined retail giant Unilever in the early 1980s. Starting in the controller's office, he moved up quickly. In 1995 he became CEO of Unox, Unilever's soup and sausage business in Holland. It was a daunting assignment, making him the new captain of a sinking ship that had to be saved or scuttled. His task of reviving sales, improving quality, and finding $5 million in cost reductions called for little short of a miracle. Success required major changes in old ways of doing things. Some of the savings would have to come from layoffs and plant closings. How could he avoid a war of mutual destruction between management and workers?

Gunning kicked off his change effort with an excursion—some fourteen hundred employees boarded buses bound for a secret destination. Many hoped for a diverting day at a theme park, but found themselves instead at an old warehouse piled with mountains of their own rejects—rotten food as far as the eye could see and the nose could smell. Quality problems long ignored were too visible and pungent to deny. It was an unforgettable experience that many remembered years later. All that waste and putrefaction brought home how deep the problems were.

That bus trip illustrates the creative confrontation that was the essence of Tex Gunning's approach to leadership. Attack tough problems directly. Take people to new and surprising places, literally as well as psychologically, that disrupt their thinking and unmoor them from old habits. Face reality head-on, but spice it with hints of drama and mystery. Historically, Dutch companies rarely laid people off because unions are so strong in Holland. Gunning took on the challenge, but he also worked hard to bring the unions on board. He communicated early and often, developed a voluntary retirement program, and enlisted area employers to find jobs for laid-off workers. He made sure that the layoffs included managers as well as workers. Otherwise, said one blue-collar worker, they would have struck.[249] Gunning's sensitivity to symbolism extended to dealings with the public as well. He aggressively courted the media, where he put less emphasis on the layoffs than on what Unilever could do with the savings. The headlines might have read, "Unilever slashes jobs." Instead, they said, "Unilever invests $150 million in its brands."[250]

Gunning and his management team worked to build a culture that was alert and agile in responding to opportunities, and they got a break that winter. Holland has an old and unique tradition called "Elfstedentocht" (loosely translated, "eleven city tour"). It doesn't happen very often, but when the canals freeze solid, everyone takes a holiday to go ice-skating. When the skaters took to the canals that January, Unox was ready. Six months earlier, the company had bought half a million orange knit hats from a vendor in China who offered a great price. Now, Unox employees were out on the ice giving away thousands of hats in the Dutch national color sporting the company logo. The result was a big media splash and tons of free advertising. "In a rare combination of planning and serendipity, putting the orange Unox hats on a nation of skaters was an inspired product promotion for a brand that was losing share and considered boring."[251]

In less than two years, the turnaround was so successful that Unilever's executives gave Gunning a new and even tougher challenge. They merged his meat business with the older and larger Van den

Bergh, a brands powerhouse that had been one Unilever's founding companies. Unox was headquartered in Holland's rural south, while Van den Bergh was situated near Unilever corporate headquarters in Rotterdam. Van den Bergh executives were dismayed and waited "in fear and horror" at the news that Gunning would be their new boss.[252] To understand the mood at Van den Bergh, imagine a group of urban sophisticates expecting to be pillaged by the Dutch equivalent of hill-billies and rednecks.

True to his nature, Gunning attacked the challenges aggressively. As one Van den Bergh marketing manager put it, "Gunning said that it should be done in a hundred days. He took the whole merger on as a personal battle. I don't know why. I'll never forget him basically saying, 'We will show how strong [Unox] is and how empty Van den Bergh is.'"[253] Not surprisingly, Gunning got off to an unpopular start. At the farewell party for his Van den Bergh predecessor, Gunning stood with arms folded and undercut the festive mood by offering a glum assessment of the business.

Business mergers fail more often than they succeed, and this one was on track to follow suit. Battle lines were forming around the company. But Gunning demonstrated an uncanny ability to make a timely shift from warrior to wizard. Only a few months after the merger, in March 1997, he convened the new organization's first-ever "Learning Conference." Two thousand employees came together for a multimedia extravaganza that began with data and ended with candles. The theme was "Competing for the Future," and the plan-ners' charge was to design a conference that was both "intellectually convincing and emotionally appealing."[254] Backed by colorful and provocative slides on a huge screen, Gunning opened with a detailed picture of the business situation, including a frank review of poor operating efficiencies in the factories. Much of it was a revelation for Van den Bergh staff, who had never known so much about the busi-ness or the boss's thinking. Gunning brought everyone to the precipice, where they all wondered, OK, now what? Then he grabbed the microphone, stepped back from the podium, and dramatically told the audience he could not solve the problems. The future, he told them, was in their hands. That was the signal for groups to go to work. The atmosphere was "very intense—a bowl of energy."[255] After hours of work sessions and trust-building activities, the conference ended with everyone standing together holding candles. The emotions were palpable and the symbolic message was clear to everyone there— each of us can make a contribution, but we need to work together.

The conference was only an early step in a multipronged change strategy. One prong was clarifying the mission. "Index 100," which called for protecting every percentage point of existing sales, became an energizing and powerful stretch goal in the face of a declining market. A second prong was structural change, establishing a clearer distinction between "value creation" (product development and marketing) and "value delivery" (sales and distribution). A third prong was an expanded training effort with an emphasis on people skills. Covey training became a merit badge that everyone wanted to earn. Still another prong was an emphasis on overthrowing an authoritarian past and freeing up leadership at every level. This worked almost too well, unleashing a group of managers who became known as the "angry young men" to revolt against their general manager. Gunning worked with both sides in search of a peace agreement, but ultimately, the general manager left and three of the angry young men were put in place as a leadership troika for the foods business.

That revolution, though ultimately successful, convinced Gunning that the organization was beginning to pay too high a price for the change and conflict, running a risk of becoming a dangerous and unhappy war zone. That was one stimulus to a fifth prong of his strategy—a series of efforts to develop deeper levels of caring, understanding, and commitment among managers and workers. "Reconnecting with people" became the theme for 1998, triggering a number of exotic and challenging off-site events. It kicked off in February with a leadership retreat in the Ardennes Forest (the harsh and wintry locale where some 180,000 Allied and German troops were killed or wounded during the Battle of the Bulge in World War II). Each of

180 designated leaders disembarked from a bus at night and received a knapsack, a warm jacket, and a flare. The flare gave light for a hike down a dark path through the woods—which led to a clearing where Gunning was waiting with a torch. The next day began with the sharing of personal life stories. Gunning went first to provide a model. As he recalled the experience:

> In the cellar of a ruin in Ardennes, I presented my emotional lifeline. It was not easy. I was in a little space in front of 180 team leaders, talking about the death of my father, an abusive stepfather, and the ups and downs of my adolescence. The silence became tangible. You touch people's hearts when you talk openly about your emotions. I will never forget a young woman in finance who was angry that I had not told my story sooner. The implicit message was, "We would have forgiven you if we could have understood you."[256]

Some in the crowd were embarrassed or skeptical, but most were deeply moved. Equally powerful was the "famous fishbowl" that opened the next day's session. Gunning and the mostly terrified management board were positioned in the middle of the room, surrounded by an audience of their subordinates. Their mission was to provide a model of open dialogue, but they were afraid that they would instead exemplify cluelessness and poor communications. Hopes and fears were both realized—openness and screwups ran about neck and neck. Audience members remembered it as the breakthrough that forever changed "the tone of company meetings."[257] Gunning saw it as the "miracle" that they needed, adding, "You can't create miracles. But you can create an environment that is inspirational, where it is safe to try things, where you can start to inquire. At the Ardennes we created that space through the lifelines and a management team exposing themselves in front of their people. Vulnerability is so powerful. You saw all the units become connected."[258]

That night, after an evening bike ride, the participants built their own campsite atop a windy hill in a cold drizzle. After erecting shelters and building fires, they ate, drank, sang, beat drums, and enjoyed deeper bonds with new friends and old. They had become "a tribe."[259]

In the years to follow, there would be many more "learning conferences" for some two thousand members of the larger tribe. There were also major events for customers, like "Big Night 1999," a party for fifty thousand retailers, grocers, spouses, and dates, complete with food, drink, song, entertainers, and discussions about the business. Leadership retreats became annual events. One year they climbed a mountain in Scotland, only to encounter miserable weather and an uninspiring opening speech from Gunning. The next day brought no improvement in the rain or the emotional tone, but day three still turned out to be miraculous. In the course of helping one another up and down Scottish hills, the leadership team developed a new theme of "Everybody together, the weakest held by the strongest."[260] In Gunning's last year heading the business, the leadership team took a culminating trip to the Jordanian desert, riding camels to the ancient city of Petra, where Gunning led a powerful change-of-command ceremony and passed the baton to his successor. "There was much to cheer: double-digit growth in previously flat markets and record profitability. Even in the flickering torchlight, those present could see the tears on Tex's cheeks as he said, 'The real miracle is that we have turned ourselves into a community.'"[261]

A PARADOXICAL LEADER

Like other leaders who combine wizard and warrior, Gunning lived at the heart of paradox. He coupled the warrior's discipline, planning, and realism with the wizard's creativity, improvisation, and imagination. He was data-driven and intuitive, tough and poetic, confrontational and intimate. Gunning's ability to live with and embrace both sides of this tension gave his leadership its transformative power.

19

PROMOTING THE DREAM

Martin Luther King Jr.

Martin Luther King Jr. was America's David, who went forth repeatedly to face the country's Goliath of white racism. King was armed with faith, courage, and the power of words. Like Joan of Arc, he came of age in a troubled and dispirited community that was struggling to throw off an oppressive yoke. Also like Joan, he did not volunteer to lead a revolution, but responded with passion and courage when he received the call.

*K*ing was twenty-five years old when he arrived in Montgomery, Alabama, in 1954. He had been recruited as a candidate for the vacant pulpit at Dexter Street Baptist Church, a small, elite church within Montgomery's black community. Dexter had cast out its last minister, and its reputation for turning over preachers was making it hard to find a replacement. King, meanwhile, was looking for a job to support his family while he finished his doctoral dissertation. He was also eager to escape the shadow of his legendary father, the long-time minister at the Ebenezer Baptist Church in Atlanta. Ebenezer's pulpit had been held by only two men in sixty years—King's grandfather, A. L. Williams, and his father, Martin Luther King Sr. King himself had been ordained and named assistant minister there while he was still in college.[262]

The young King was well aware that a storm was brewing over civil rights in America, but could not have anticipated that Montgomery would become its focal point. In December 1955, fourteen months after he took the pulpit at Dexter Street, Rosa Parks refused a bus driver's request that she give up her seat for a white rider. She was arrested and jailed for violating a city ordinance requiring racial segregation on public conveyances. Hers was not the first such incident—she was at least the third woman arrested that year for the same offense. But anger and frustration had been building in the black community, and its leaders had been waiting for the right protagonist to galvanize sentiments and goad people into action. Parks, who was the secretary of the local chapter of the NAACP, came from a solid working-class family, and was widely respected. Over the weekend following her arrest, plans were formulated for what was planned as a one-day boycott of Montgomery's buses.

King was not involved in launching that initiative, but he was already making a name for himself in Montgomery for his performance in the pulpit. "King was controlled. He never shouted. But he preached like someone who wanted to shout, and this gave him an electrifying hold over the congregation. Though still a boy to many of his older listeners, he had the commanding air of a burning sage."[263]

The bus boycott that began on Monday was a total success. Throughout the city, buses rolled empty except for white riders. That afternoon, a group of black leaders, mostly clergy, met to plan for a mass meeting scheduled that evening. Whether because of his gifts, or because he was new and had little political baggage, or because more senior leaders were reluctant to take on a hard and dangerous job, King was elected to head a new organization—the Montgomery Improvement Association—that would coordinate the effort. He raced home for dinner and had less than half an hour to prepare to address the audience at the evening's meeting.

It was a huge crowd, overflowing the Holt Street Church and out into the grounds, with loudspeakers for the people outside. When King took the pulpit, he began slowly. His audience was supportive but not yet enthusiastic. He almost lost them with a tortured and long-winded analysis of the city ordinance. But then he began to talk about Rosa Parks, saying that no one could doubt her character and Christian commitment. She was arrested, he said, only because she refused to give up her seat. The crowd was coming alive, and after a long pause, King delivered the clincher, "And you know, my friends, there comes a time when people get tired of being trampled over by the iron feet of oppression." The crowd exploded in a wave of enthusiasm. "Suddenly the individual responses dissolved into a rising cheer and applause exploded beneath the cheer. The startling noise rolled on and on, like a wave that refused to break."[264] The boycott had found the leader it needed.

In the beginning, no one imagined that Rosa Parks's defiance would turn into anything very significant. A similar effort in Baton Rouge, Louisiana, two years earlier had fallen apart after only two weeks. Montgomery's white power structure mobilized quickly to bring economic and police power to bear on the mostly poor black community. King was twice arrested and jailed, and his home was firebombed. King hurried home, verified that his wife and baby daughter were unharmed, and then went out to his front porch to quiet an angry crowd of supporters. After assuring them about his family, the preacher in him reached full force. Even if he were stopped, he told the crowd, the movement would go on because it was right and God was with them.[265]

The bus boycott lasted more than a year, ultimately producing a victory in the U.S. Supreme Court, which struck down state and local laws in Alabama that mandated racial segregation. It turned King into a celebrity before he was thirty—a man known nationally and internationally as a powerful champion of civil rights. King took on the new role eagerly. He traveled hundreds of thousands of miles a year to preach and speak around the United States. He traveled to India to study Gandhi's philosophy of nonviolence. He and a group of fellow preachers founded the Southern Christian Leadership Conference, which put massive energy into a voter registration drive. All these efforts continued to build King's reputation, but made little dent in the basic issues of segregation and injustice. The registration drive was largely a failure. Whites in the south were resisting at every turn, and whites in the north were mostly ignoring the problem. After a successful first act, King struggled to define what to do next. Then fate handed him the opportunity he needed.

On Monday, February 1, 1960, four freshmen at North Carolina A & T University made a spontaneous decision to go to the Woolworth's in downtown Greensboro and sit at the whites-only lunch counter. They had no plan and little idea of what to expect, but were surprised to find that the Woolworth's management floundered, confused about how to respond. As one of the four students recalled, "Seeing the policeman pace the aisle and not be able to do anything, I think that gave us more strength, more encouragement, than anything else on day one."[266] The waitress wouldn't serve them, but they sat there all afternoon, and promised to come back the next morning. They did, joined by nineteen more students, and the number grew to eighty-five on Wednesday. Sit-ins had been tried from time to time for more than a decade, but none of the rest had caught on. Now the time was right. By the end of the week, sit-ins had spread to cities across the south.

As with the Montgomery bus boycott, King did not initiate, but he immediately saw the opportunity. At the initial meeting of the newly formed Student Nonviolent Coordinating Committee (SNCC) in April, he became the first established leader to speak in praise of the students. "What is fresh, what is new in your fight," he said, "is the fact that it was initiated, led, and sustained by students. What is new is that American students have come of age. You now take your honored places in the world-wide struggle for freedom."[267]

As the sit-ins spread, the vehemence of white opposition intensified. King's own position became more difficult when he was indicted by the state of Alabama for tax evasion—becoming the first person in Alabama history to be so indicted. There was little doubt that the indictment was a reprisal for King's leadership rather than his tax returns, but he was still dismayed and discouraged, worried about the possibility that his credibility might be undermined. He canceled speaking engagements, but then reversed his position and decided it was essential to continue.

Over the next few years, a similar pattern repeated itself. King was not the initiator of new civil rights protests, but he was the champion who would stand up to the white power structure, the priest who was called in to provide blessings, and the poet who could craft a message that was persuasive to a broader national audience. This was true of the freedom rides in 1961, when activists began to test a 1960 Supreme Court ruling that segregation in interstate travel was illegal. King doubted the wisdom of the initiative, but when riders were greeted with arrests and violence, he led rallies and became a leading spokesman defending their protests. Later the same year, a movement arose in Albany, Georgia, seeking to end all segregation in the city. After more than five hundred protestors were jailed and negotiations with city officials reached a standstill, King was invited to reinvigorate the movement. King traveled to the city twice, and was jailed each time. Though the "Albany Movement" achieved modest victories, King concluded in retrospect that the effort had taken on too much, leaving disappointment in its wake.

The lesson served him well when he and the SCLC leadership decided to join protests already under way in Birmingham, Alabama. The Albany experience taught King to concentrate on a single target. In Birmingham, that target became the business community because it was vulnerable to economic boycotts from the black community.[268]

The Birmingham campaign began in the spring of 1963. The police arrested protestors in large numbers, and King soon found himself facing one of his perennial quandaries. He had announced that he and close associate Ralph Abernathy would lead a protest the next day, fully expecting to be jailed as a result. But some of his colleagues pressured him not to go, arguing that they were out of bail money, and needed him to get more support from the outside world. King agonized, as he often did, but then concluded he had no choice: "Then my tortured mind leaped beyond the Gaston motel, past the city jail, past the city and state lines, and I thought of the twenty million black people who dreamed that someday they might be able to cross the Red Sea of injustice and find their way into the promised land of integration and freedom. There was no longer room for doubt."[269] King was arrested, and spent a week in jail, the first twenty-four hours in solitary confinement. This stay produced his famous letter from a Birmingham jail. To keep the pressure on, organizers recruited high school students, producing one of the most memorable events in the civil rights struggle:

On 2 May 1963, over one thousand black children descended upon Birmingham. Close to nine hundred students were arrested, but a reserve army of close to twenty-five hundred demonstrated the following day. [Birmingham police chief and former mayor] Bull Connor, who had up until this point "restrained" from violence against protesters, ordered firemen to use their hoses on the protesters and onlookers. As the youth fled from the power of the hoses, Connor directed officers and their dogs to pursue them. John Lewis noted the power of this incident: "We didn't fully comprehend at first what was happening. We were witnessing police violence and brutality Birmingham-style: unfortunately for Bull Connor, so was the rest of the world." As the clashes between nonviolent protesters and police made headlines across the country—with pictures of policemen bending over women with raised clubs, children marching up to the aggressive police dogs, and pressure hoses sweeping bodies into the streets—the movement reached a new level of visibility.[270]

The violence in Birmingham set the stage for a climactic moment in the Civil Rights movement—the March on Washington in August 1963—at which King delivered the most famous oration of the twentieth century, his "I have a dream" speech. The magic of the speech was in the way King framed the dream, as one "deeply rooted in the American dream." It might have been enough to argue that it was fair and just to give black citizens the same rights as whites. But King went a critical step further in arguing that America had been founded on the premise that "all men are created equal," and that in signing the Declaration of Independence and the Constitution, the founding fathers had signed "a promissory note to which every American was to fall heir," a note that would give them "upon demand, the riches of freedom and the security of justice." "If America is to be a great nation," he summarized, "this must become true." In short, King's was a dream of justice for black citizens, but it went to a deeper level, asking if America would keep its promises and live up to its most cherished values. That was what made his message so powerful and inescapable for white America.[271]

FUSING POWER AND MAGIC

It many ways, it is hard to imagine situations more different than those of Thomas J. Watson, Lou Gerstner, Joan of Arc, Tex Gunning, and Martin Luther King Jr. Yet we see a similar dramatic arc in all these stories. Each was an outsider entering a frustrated, dispirited group. Each encountered skepticism and hostility, but gradually built credibility and even devotion among many of their constituents. Each was remarkably creative, bringing new ways to understand the situation and its possibilities. Each was passionately committed to transformative goals for the chosen group, whether IBM, war-torn France, Unilever's foods business, or America's citizens of color.

Given the many differences among these leaders, it is remarkable to find so many similarities in the script they followed.

1. *Transform the existing reality with a wake-up call for the status quo and a vision of future success.*

Wizards transform by turning the kaleidoscope to create a new picture of the present and the future. Watson brought the best of his old boss to his new company to create an inspiring image for his sales force. To a French court that was losing hope as well as battles, Joan brought a promise to make the dauphin the true king of France. She achieved it within a year. Martin Luther King Jr. became the most eloquent and compelling voice of the dream of equality.

2. *Lead with symbols and symbolic events.*

Watson relied on dress codes, slogans, ritual, and song to inspire his new company. Joan used prayer, priests, armor, and flags in pursuit of a goal that was symbolic as much as military. Gunning relied on ceremonial events that took people out of their daily routine and confronted them with new challenges and opportunities. King's leadership was expressed through his mastery of symbolic language and his willingness to put himself on the line for his cause.

3. *Stay focused and sustain a sense of urgency.*

Watson was tireless in building a culture that supported IBM's commitment to sales and service. Lou Gerstner, stunned by lethargy in IBM's senior ranks, focused on rebuilding the culture around its historic values. Joan was entirely devoted to establishing the dauphin as the true king, and then driving the English out of France. After achieving the first, she stubbornly pursued the second purpose even as her allies hesitated. Gunning and King were both focused and stubborn in pursuing their respective visions.

4. *Persist.*

Discouragement and reversals are part of any change program and any leader's life. Watson's career began with a series of failures, but he heeded the lessons and kept going. All of these leaders encountered resistance but refused to take no for an answer.

5. *Take risks and model courage.*

All these leaders showed remarkable willingness to put themselves, their reputations, and, in the cases of Joan of Arc and Martin Luther King Jr., life itself on the line. In battle, Joan carried her standard rather than her sword because she was there to inspire, not to fight. Wounded multiple times, she kept returning to the fray. King was harassed, jailed, physically attacked, and ultimately assassinated. Gunning made himself personally open and vulnerable in a way that often startled his coworkers.

All these leaders had great self-confidence that sometimes bordered on arrogance, yet each ultimately put service to a larger cause above personal gains or losses. All had confidence in their people—confidence that, working together, they could mobilize to achieve miraculous things. And each showed remarkable courage by standing up in the face of powerful opponents and taking great personal risks. All combined qualities of authentic wizard and principled warrior in ways that enabled them to work powerful magic.

Some of these leaders were also comparatively young. The traditional image of a wizard is a wizened old man with flowing white hair and beard. But Joan of Arc was a legend at seventeen, Martin Luther King Jr. at twenty-six. Maturity helps in attaining wisdom, but it can come much earlier to those who bring creativity, passion, and faith to their work.

20

ENHANCING THE WIZARD AND WARRIOR WITHIN

The qualities of great leaders are characteristics of mind, soul, heart, and skill that evolve over a lifetime of learning and experience. There is no quick and easy route to leadership effectiveness, and reading many books on the topic provides no guarantee that you will become a better leader. Yet ideas make a difference—if they change how you see and engage your world, and lead you to embark on a journey that creates new learning and new opportunities.

*I*f you have read this book carefully and thoughtfully, we hope it has stimulated you to reflect on how you approach leadership and prompted you to inventory your strengths, vulnerabilities, and inclinations as both wizard and warrior. You may have begun to sketch out your own learning agenda. In this chapter, we discuss ideas and directions for developing your knowledge of yourself and your ability to fill the roles of both wizard and warrior.

DEVELOPING WARRIOR HEART AND SKILL

As is clear from examples like Abraham Lincoln and Nelson Mandela, you need not like war to be a warrior. Albert Einstein described himself as a "militant pacifist" who was "willing to fight for peace," and repeatedly took courageous action on behalf of his antiwar sentiments.[272] Warriors include physicians who risk their lives to provide medical care in a war zone, radical priests who battle to bring justice to their people, and mothers who fight to get services for a disabled child. To be a warrior, you need only a cause for which you will give your all.

But when something dear to you is threatened, you must be willing to fight with passion and conviction, and you must fight to win. If you have little taste for battle and turn away from conflict, whether from fear, distaste, or principle, face that reality directly. Pretending to be what you are not is pointless. You need to decide if this is something to overcome or accept. Not everyone is a warrior. You may have other strengths and other ways of leading. But know that it is a vulnerability. If your group faces real threats from real enemies, your distaste for combat will almost inevitably prove costly, if not catastrophic, for you, your people, and your purposes. Albert Einstein earned the scorn of many of his fellow pacifists when he urged European nations to be prepared to defend themselves against Adolph Hitler's Germany. Einstein had studied the Nazis closely before emigrating to America in 1933 and harbored no romantic illusion that Hitler would be deterred by moral suasion.

Against the possibility that conflict will come your way, you have several options. One is to hope that good fortune smiles upon you, and that the time never comes when you must stand and fight. In some times and circumstances, that is plausible. In others, it is a dangerous delusion.

A second option is hire a warrior—a champion who can do for you what you cannot do for yourself. President Abraham Lincoln spent the early years of the Civil War in a frustrated search for a general who would take the battle to the enemy, despite the often terrible costs. In his disappointment, Lincoln sometimes succumbed to the temptation to micromanage the war effort. But he knew it was not his job and that he was not particularly good at it. He finally found his man in General Ulysses S. Grant, of whom Lincoln said, "I cannot spare this man. He fights." Ronald Reagan was more wizard than warrior, but he was supported by a number of political spear-carriers (such as Lee Atwater and his protégé Karl Rove) who loved combat.

The third option is to develop a warrior's heart. The skills of a warrior can unquestionably be taught and learned, but warrior heart is harder to develop. It comes naturally to some people, such as the toxic and relentless warriors whose passion for victory propels them enthusiastically into battle. For principled warriors, it must be found in a cause important enough to justify the costs of combat. For many leaders, heart develops over time through experiences that test their courage and strength in the face of rigorous challenge and worthy competitors. Those experiences come in many forms.

Militaries around the globe have shown that an effective training regimen can covert young men (and, increasingly, women), fresh from farms or factory floors, with no skill or experience in military arts, into effective warriors in a year or two. On the eve of World War II, the U.S. Army was a small professional force of less than 200,000 soldiers. Five years later, more than 8 million G.I.s were fighting and winning around the globe.

Military experience is a powerful way to test and develop oneself as a warrior, and for some it will be the best way. But there are many other paths, all involving willingness to enter competitive arenas, test one's capacities, and develop skills and courage. Athletics have been a powerful formative experience for many leaders. One persuasive rationale for equal opportunity for men and women to participate in competitive sports is that they offer an arena for developing warrior skills and heart. But the competition need not be physical. One can learn to be a more effective competitor in intellectual and social arenas as well—running for office or participating in electoral campaigns, joining a debate team, even learning the intricacies of bridge or Texas hold'em. The key is to engage and learn from experiences that test your capacities as a warrior.

DEVELOPING WIZARD SPIRIT AND WISDOM

When we avoid the warrior in ourselves, it is often because we fear and sometimes loathe some of our darker, less acceptable feelings such as anger, selfishness, cowardice, or desires for wealth and power. The wizard is another matter. We wonder if we even have the capacity for magic, and fear a role that seems mysterious and alien. Warriors must overcome fear of battle. Wizards must transcend fear of the irrational and the unknown. Warriors must learn to fight. Wizards need immersion in subtler arts of magic, illusion, imagination, and creation.

If the wizard's magic and mystery are foreign to your aspirations and your sense of self, decide if this is something you can accept or need to overcome. If you choose acceptance, focus on leading in other ways. You may be effective as a warrior. You may be an analyst and conceptualizer who is best as an intellectual leader. You could also be a people person who leads best through sensitivity and caring.

You can also choose to ally yourself with a magician—or the magician may come looking for you. Oprah Winfrey is a magician with an art for eliciting responses from her audiences that almost no one else in television can do. But it is harder for her to adopt the warrior role. Early in her career, she concluded that she was giving away too much because her agent was too nice. When several different people at her TV station told her what a wonderful guy her agent was, she fired him and hired a warrior named Jeffrey Jacobs, a Chicago lawyer with a reputation. "I'd heard that Jeff is a piranha. I like that. Piranha is good," Winfrey said.[273] It was good for Winfrey. Jacobs worked the deal that enabled her go nationwide—and ultimately to knock off the king of daytime talk, Phil Donahue.

How do wizards become wizardly? Books and legend consistently provide a simple answer: embark on your journey, follow your bliss, and, with luck, find a mentor, a wise magician who can guide you to your spiritual center. You will never get there by staying home, relaxing into the mundane, and repeating the same experiences day after day.

In World War I, Ray Kroc, the architect of the McDonald's restaurant chain, drove ambulances in the same company as Walt Disney. Kroc later talked about the differences between the two of them. "He was always drawing pictures while the rest of us were chasing girls. Therein lies a lesson, because his drawings have gone on forever—and most of those girls are dead now."[274] Kroc and Disney had much in common. Both had passions early in their career—Disney for drawing and Kroc for the food business. But their dreams were clouded and neither knew where their journey would take them. Both had false starts. At one low point, Disney lived in his office, subsisting mostly on beans straight from the can. But he and Kroc both kept moving to new places and experiences. Disney worked designing stationery, making program covers for movie theaters, and drawing ads for small businesses before he finally left hometown Kansas City to try his luck in Hollywood. Kroc went through paper cups and milk shake machines before finally discovering his dream in buns and burgers. But what a discovery it was. In his words, "It takes a certain kind of mind to see beauty in a hamburger bun."[275] Disney and Kroc were not born as magicians, and neither had any foreknowledge of his destiny. But each followed his bliss, experimented, and kept moving until the dream finally began to crystallize.

Though the learning paths for wizard and warrior are distinct, there are commonalities. Self-knowledge is vital for both. So are skill and discipline. Both benefit from teachers, masters of the art, who can help them acquire skills, deepen their knowledge of the art and of themselves, and gain control over powers that can cause great damage if misdirected or misused. Both need passion and commitment to their chosen path, along with the determination to keep moving, even when the way is hard and the destination is unclear. You just gotta believe and have faith. Walt Whitman got it right in "Passage to India":

> *Have we not stood here like trees in the*
> *ground long enough?*
> *Sail forth—steer for the deep waters only,*
> *Reckless O soul, exploring, I with thee*
> *and thou with me,*
> *For we are bound where mariner has*
> *not yet dared to go,*
> *And we will risk the ship, ourselves,*
> *and all.*[276]

21

THE SWORD
AND THE WAND

When an enemy is at the gate, we want warriors to protect us from danger and defeat our enemies. When the threat is within—a failure of imagination or will—we need a wizard. The wizard can help us see possibilities never imagined and do things we would not have believed possible. Those who have found neither the wizard's spirit nor the warrior's ways within themselves have little chance of leadership success. Even talent, energy, and persistence may not save their initiatives from deteriorating into bureaucratic tyranny or ineffectual wheedling. Ideally, leaders need both—the warrior's courage and skill in combat alloyed with the wizard's imagination and magic.

*M*uch leaders are rare because they must embrace paradox and develop mastery in very different realms. If we look at the differences between these two archetypal figures, we find that they are engaged in a multidimensional dance of opposites:

	WARRIOR	WIZARD
Wields:	Sword	Wand
Primary task:	Defeat enemies	Create possibilities
Viewpoint:	Accept reality: see what is	Reframe reality: see what might be
Learning mode:	Sensing	Intuiting
Main support:	Strategy, strength, courage	Insight, wisdom, magic
Epistemology:	Pragmatic materialism	Imaginative idealism
Realm:	Physical world	Metaphysical and spiritual world
Needed when:	The enemy is at the gates	The enemy is within
Prepares for future:	Developing strategy	Creating vision
Prepares for action:	Training, arming	Study, spiritual reflection
Leadership roles:	Commander, champion, advocate	Priest, counselor, shaman
Vulnerabilities:	Failure of skill or will	Loss of faith and magic

The combination of the two is paradoxical, but we know that it is possible from leaders we have studied who have changed history in large or small ways. Leaders who make a difference have regularly combined the warrior's instinct for combat with the wizard's imagination and foresight. To combine the two, leaders must have an extraordinary ability to embrace both sides of tensions and polarities others see as unbridgeable opposites. They must:

1. *Wield both sword and wand: know how to create as well as defend.*

Leaders need the sword to defend a group and its way of life, and they need the wand to create and transform cultural values and ways.

2. *Accept current reality, and challenge it because they see its possibilities.*

Leaders need to see the world both as it is and as it might be, while being clear about the difference between the two.

3. *Learn by sensing and intuiting.*

Great leaders need great powers of observation—they must see, hear, feel, and smell acutely and perceptively. They also need great powers of intuition—they must be able to burrow beneath the surface veneer and recognize underlying forces and possibilities that lie beyond the senses.

4. *Be both strategists and visionaries.*

They need the analytic brilliance of the great strategist as well as the imagination and insight of the visionary.

5. *Combine the power of the commander and the courage of the champion with the wisdom of the counselor and the magical powers of the shaman.*

This paradoxical combination is difficult, but we have seen in the preceding chapters that great leaders find ways to do it.

HENRY AND THE RUBBER RAILROAD

Henry Kaiser built roads, dams (including Hoover, Boulder, and Grand Coulee), ships (some fifteen hundred to support the war effort in World War II), Hawaiian resorts, and a new model of health care (Kaiser Permanente). He didn't do it by being a patient man.

One of his managers on a construction job suggested that the world wouldn't end if the crews didn't meet one of Kaiser's typically ambitious deadlines. "After all, Mr. Kaiser, Rome wasn't built in a day."

"That's because I wasn't there," Kaiser rejoined.[277]

Kaiser loved challenges and never shrank from a battle. After Kaiser's group lost to another bidder on the contract to build the Shasta dam in California, he bid for and won the contract to supply the cement, even though he'd never been in the cement business. Then his problems began. The California cement cartel was angry at being underbid by an upstart who didn't even have a cement plant. The cartel used its close connections to the Southern Pacific Railway to ensure that Kaiser was quoted exorbitant freight rates for transporting cement to the site. Kaiser's many appeals to the railroad made no dent. Then one of his employees suggested that they build their own conveyor. Kaiser dismissed the idea as impractical. The employee taunted him, asking, "Are you chicken?" That was all Kaiser needed. He built a ten-mile "rubber railroad," the longest conveyer belt in the world. It went up and down ridges, across rivers, creeks, roads, and, to Kaiser's great pleasure, across the Southern Pacific's rail line. It saved Kaiser about a third off the railroad's rates and got him into a profitable cement business. "Losing out on the construction of the Shasta Dam was one of the best things that ever happened to us," he said.[278]

Kaiser was both wizard and warrior, and the case of his rubber railroad reminds us of fundamental lessons for leaders. Keep the larger purpose in mind. Persist in the face of opposition and obstacle. Listen to your troops. Hold to your purpose, but be flexible about means, always looking for new ways to achieve your purposes. Take prudent risks. When things get tough, redouble your courage and

your determination. Kaiser brought all the essential leadership qualities of courage, faith, creativity, and passion that are characteristic
of leaders who embody both sides of the wizard/warrior tension. It
worked for him, as it will for others.

BILL AND SOPHIE

Polarization in American politics in recent years has taken a toll on
those who have been elected to the presidency. In the case of former
President Bill Clinton, almost no one is neutral. Americans generally
fall into one of three groups: those who never liked him, those who
used to like him but don't anymore, and die-hard supporters. A similar distribution of sentiment has evolved for Clinton's successor, President George W. Bush. But if we cut through the political fog, each
offers leadership lessons. We already examined Bush as a warrior in
an earlier chapter. Clinton, in contrast, was a better wizard than warrior. Unlike the highly focused Bush, Clinton lacked warrior discipline,
and his eagerness to please drove him to seek harmony rather than
conflict.

Yet he could move into the warrior role when the stakes were
high enough. One example occurred during the budget crisis in 1995.
A duel between the Clinton White House and Newt Gingrich in the
House of Representatives left the U.S. government without a budget
and twice forced a shutdown of nonessential functions. On the second
occasion, the Republican Congressional leadership asked to meet with
the president. Some of Clinton's staff tried to head off the meeting
because, as one put it, "You just can't put Bill Clinton alone in a room
with an opponent. That's not what he's good at. He'll just give away
everything."[279]

But on this occasion, Clinton was ready for battle. In his mind,
the budget the Republicans wanted to pass would do too much damage to the poor and vulnerable. When Texas Republican Dick Armey
complained that the president was trying to scare his mother-in-law
about Medicare, Clinton came back hard: "I don't know about your

mother-in-law,' Clinton hissed, 'but if your budget passes, thousands of poor people are going to suffer because of your Medicaid cuts. I will never sign your Medicaid cuts. I don't care if I go down to five percent in the polls. If you want your budget passed, you're going to have to put someone else in this chair.'"[280]

Clinton held the line and achieved a political victory that helped him get reelected the following year. But by nature he preferred the wizard's role. He was a master of symbols, an entertaining storyteller, and had an extraordinary talent for energizing supporters and making a personal connection with them. Political reporter Joe Klein, who started following Bill Clinton's career in 1989, came to know him well—his strengths as well as his foibles—by the time Clinton first campaigned for the presidency in 1992. But Clinton could still surprise:

> In the spring of 1992, in the midst of the New York primary, I dragged my five-year-old daughter, Sophie, to see Bill Clinton speak at a town meeting at Co-op City in the Bronx. It was a raucous affair, a barrage of angry, detailed questions from retired trade unionists and other assorted skeptics. Clinton was in the midst of a rough patch, under assault from the New York tabloids and also from the liberal intelligentsia. I had piled on, too, with a column in *New York* magazine about the fudges and inconsistencies in his campaign. But when Clinton saw Sophie standing with me as he made his way out of the hall, he came over, squatted down, put a big hand on my daughter's shoulder, and said, "Sophie, I know that your father hasn't been home much these past few months. He's been with me . . . but he talks about you *all the time.*[281]

There's magic at work here. It has two of the central characteristics of magical performances. First, it produces awe and wonder: How did he do that? A lot of reporters, many with children, were following Clinton at the time. How did he know Sophie by name? How did he know she was wondering why her dad was away so much? How could he be so genially charming with the daughter of someone who'd just raked him over the coals in the midst of a tough primary battle? Second, it transforms the situation, magically transporting people from one world (in this case, the tension and combat of politics and the media) to another (a place of caring, family, and intimacy). As is always true of magic, skeptics can raise questions: Does the wizard actually care about Sophie, or merely about soft-soaping a political reporter? Is he authentic or phony? Is the enchantment we feel a blessing or a trap?

Few magical performances will enchant everyone, but we need magic more than ever. In Clinton's Sophie choice are simple lessons that all leaders can take to heart—if they bring focus, attention, and a commitment to leadership as a calling. Look for ways to surprise constituents by showing them possibilities they never imagined. Take them to a new place, a deeper, more inspiring magical world. Do it through action, not just talk. Look for the transformational opportunities that exist everywhere and in every moment.

We can attain the warrior's power and the wizard's magic with effort, passion, and continual learning. If we want to lead and know what we want to achieve or build, we have all we need to embark on our leadership journey.

The ideas and examples in this book can serve as signposts along the way. Don't worry about stumbling or falling. That's often where you learn the most. As the Wizard of Oz said to the Cowardly Lion, every living thing is afraid in the face of danger. Courage is the ability to move ahead anyway. All you need is confidence in yourself and passion for your cause.

NOTES

1. L. G. Bolman and T. E. Deal, "Leadership and Management Effectiveness: A Multi-Frame, Multi-Sector Analysis," *Human Resource Management,* 1991, *30,* 509–534.

2. "Leaders and Revolutionaries: Twenty People Who Helped Define the Political and Social Fabric of Our Times," *Time,* Dec. 8, 1998. Available online: http://www.time.com/time/time100/leaders/index.html. Access date: Oct. 25, 2005.

3. Jim Hager, personal communication to authors.

4. Quoted in A. Applebaum and R. Blow, "The Power and the Personality," *New Journal,* Feb. 28, 1986, p. 17.

5. N. Floyd and L. Bolman, "Yale University [C]," Cambridge, Mass.: Institute for Educational Management, Harvard University, 1987, pp. 8–9.

6. R. M. Nixon, *In the Arena: A Memoir of Victory, Defeat, and Renewal,* New York: Simon & Schuster, 1990.

7. D. Gergen, *Eyewitness to Power: The Essence of Leadership, Nixon to Clinton,* New York: Touchstone, 2000, pp. 30–31.

8. Gergen, 2000, p. 31.

9. Vatican News, "Mother Teresa of Calcutta (1910–1997)," 2003. Available online: http://www.vatican.va/news_services/liturgy/saints/ns_lit_doc_2003 1019_madre-teresa_en.html. Access date: Nov. 28, 2005.

10. A. Chatterjee, *Mother Teresa: The Final Verdict,* Kolkata, India: Meteor, 2003; C. Hitchens, *The Missionary Position: Mother Teresa in Theory and Practice,* London: Verso, 1997.

11. L. G. Bolman and T. E. Deal, *Reframing Organizations: Artistry, Choice, and Leadership,* San Francisco: Jossey-Bass: 2003.

12. Bolman and Deal, 1991.

13. E. Hamilton, *Mythology: Timeless Tales of Gods and Heroes,* New York: Warner, 1999, p. 34; originally published in 1942.

14. C. Hedges, *War Is a Force That Gives Us Meaning,* New York: Anchor, 2002.

15. M.F.R. Kets de Vries, *Leaders, Fools, and Imposters,* New York: Universe, 2003; B. Kellerman, *Bad Leadership: What It Is, Why It Happens, Why It Matters,* Boston: Harvard Business School Press, 2004; J. Lipman-Blumen, *The Allure of Toxic Leaders: Why We Follow Destructive Bosses and Corrupt Politicians—and How We Can Survive Them,* Oxford, England: Oxford University Press, 2005.

16. Kets de Vries, 2003.

17. Kellerman, 2004.

18. Kellerman, 2004.

19. R. Hammer, *The Helmsleys: The Rise and Fall of Harry and Leona,* London: Penguin, 1999; Kellerman, 2004.

20. J. A. Byrne, "The Shredder: Did CEO Dunlap Save Scott Paper—or Just Pretty It Up?" *Business Week,* Jan. 15, 1996.

21. C. Lasch, *The Culture of Narcissism: American Life in an Age of Diminishing Expectations,* revised edition, New York: Norton, 1991, p. 10.

22. K. Blanchard and S. Johnson, *The One Minute Manager,* New York: Morrow, 1982.

23. S. Ambrose, *The Supreme Commander: The War Years of Dwight D. Eisenhower,* New York: Doubleday, 1970.

24. Ambrose, 1970.

25. M. Klein, *The Change Makers: From Carnegie to Gates, How the Great Entrepreneurs Transformed Ideas into Industries,* New York: Time Books, 2003, p. 109.

26. H. W. Brands, *Masters of Enterprise: Giants of American Business from John Jacob Astor and J.P. Morgan to Bill Gates and Oprah Winfrey,* New York: Free Press, 1999.

27. Brands, 1999, p. 20.

28. Klein, 2003, p. 110.

29. S. Manes and P. Andrews, *Gates,* New York: Touchstone, 1994; G. P. Zachary, *Showstopper! The Breakneck Race to Create Windows NT and the Next Generation at Microsoft,* New York: Free Press, 1994.

30. D. Bank, *Breaking Windows: How Bill Gates Fumbled the Future of Microsoft,* New York: Free Press, 2001.

31. B. Schlender, "Is Wintel Out of Gas?" *Fortune,* Jan. 10, 2005, p. 54.

32. P. Burrows, *Backfire: Carly Fiorina's High-Stakes Battle for the Soul of Hewlett-Packard,* New York: Wiley, 2003.

33. Burrows, 2003.

34. P. Burrows and P. Elstrom, "HP's Carly Fiorina: The Boss," *Business Week,* Aug. 2, 1999, pp. 76–84.

35. Burrows and Elstrom, 1999.

36. Burrows, 2003.

37. E. Laise, "Is This the Most Influential Man on Wall Street?" *SmartMoney.Com,* Oct. 16, 2002. Available online: http://wwwsmartmoney.com/mag/index.cfm?story=oct02-influential. Access date: Nov. 28, 2005.

38. I. Fried, "HP board slams Walter Hewlett," C/Net New.Com, 2002. Available online: http://news.com.com/2100-1001-818687.html. Access date: Nov. 28, 2005.

39. D. Gergen, "Stubborn Kind of Fellow," *Compass,* Fall 2003, pp. 14–17 & 21; quote on p. 14.

40. Gergen, 2003, p. 15.

41. Ambrose, 1970, p. 344.

42. C. J. Chivers, "How Ukraine's Top Spies Changed the Nation's Path," *New York Times,* Jan. 17, 2005, pp. A1 & A6. Available online: http://www.nytimes.com/2005/01/17/international/europe/17ukraine.html?oref=login&th. Access date: Oct. 27, 2005 (subscription required).

43. Chivers, 2005.

44. C. M. Province, *The Unknown Patton,* New York: Bonanza, 1983, p. 32.

45. Ambrose, 1970, p. 187.

46. W. L. Miller, *Lincoln's Virtues: An Ethical Biography*, New York: Vintage, 2003.

47. C. Sandburg, *Abraham Lincoln: The War Years, Vol. 4*, New York: Harcourt Brace, 1939, p. 94.

48. Sandburg, Vol. 1, 1939, pp. 132–133.

49. Sandburg, Vol. 1, 1939, p. 134.

50. Miller, 2003, p. 43.

51. Joshua Shenk, in *Lincoln's Melancholy: How Depression Challenged a President and Fueled His Greatness* (New York: Houghton Mifflin, 2005), argues that the skills Lincoln developed to manage his melancholy were a part of his greatness.

52. Miller, 2003, p. 328.

53. A. Lincoln, "Speech of Hon. Abraham Lincoln Delivered in Springfield, Saturday Evening, July 17, 1858. (Mr. Douglas Was Not Present.)." Available online: http://www.bartleby.com/251/1006.html. Access date: Nov. 28, 2005.

54. S. A. Douglas, "Speech of Senator Douglas, delivered at Bloomington, Ill., July 16, 1858 (Mr. Lincoln Was Present.)." Available online: http://www.bartleby.com/251/1004.html. Access date: Oct. 27, 2005.

55. Miller, 2003, p. 350.

56. W. Cooper (Ed.), "James Buchanan Biography: A Life in Brief." Available online: http://www.americanpresident.org/history/jamesbuchanan/biography/LifeinBrief.common.shtml. Access date: Oct. 27, 2005.

57. A. Brink, "Nelson Mandela," *Time Magazine*, Apr. 13, 1998. Available online: http://www.time.com/time/time100/leaders/profile/mandela.html. Access date: Oct. 27, 2005.

58. B. Ortega, *In Sam We Trust: The Untold Story of Sam Walton and How Wal-Mart Is Devouring America*, New York: Times Business, 1998.

59. Klein, 2003, p. 110.

60. Quoted in W. Safire and L. Safir, *Leadership*, New York: Firestone, 1991, p. 62.

61. C. F. Brower, "George C. Marshall: A Study in Character." Paper presented at the 1999 Joint Services Conference on Professional Ethics, Springfield, Va., Jan. 28–29, 1999, p. 5. Available online: http://www.usafa.af.mil/jscope/JSCOPE99/Brower99.html. Access date: Oct. 27, 2005.

62. C. von Clausewitz, *On War* (M. E. Howard and P. Paret, trans.), Princeton, N.J.: Princeton University Press, 1989, p. 193; originally published in 1833.

63. Sun Tzu, *The Art of War* (L. Giles, trans.), New York: Dover, 2002, p. 3; originally written about 500 BCE.

64. Clausewitz, 1989 [1833], pp. 88–89.

65. Ambrose, 1970, p. 608.

66. Mao Tse-tung, *On Guerrilla Warfare* (S. B. Griffith II, trans.), Champaign: University of Illinois Press, 2000, p. 105; originally written in 1937. (Note: This edition uses the Wade Giles system rather than pinyin for Chinese transliteration. We generally refer to its author as Mao Zedong.)

67. Klein, 2003, p. 161.

68. Klein, 2003.

69. Quoted in J. C. Carter and M. S. Finer, "Stonewall Jackson and George S. Patton: A Survey of Leadership," *Infantry Magazine*, Jan.-Feb. 2004. Available online: http://www.army.mil/professionalwriting/volumes/volume2/april_2004/4_04_1.html. Access date: Oct. 27, 2005.

70. Mao Tse-tung, 2000 [1937], p. 46.

71. Klein, 2003.

72. D. Goleman, *Emotional Intelligence: Why It Can Matter More Than IQ,* New York: Bantam, 1997.

73. Sun Tzu, 2002 [500 BCE], p. 9.

74. D. K. Goodwin, *Team of Rivals: The Political Genius of Abraham Lincoln,* New York: Simon & Schuster, 2005.

75. Goodwin, 2005, p. 100.

76. Sandberg, 1939, Vol. 1, p. 139.

77. Sandberg, 1939, Vol. 1, p. 181.

78. Brands, 1999, p. 255.

79. Brands, 1999, p. 251.

80. A. E. Kornblut, "Tom DeLay's Empire of Favors," *New York Times,* May 8, 2005, pp. 4-1 & 4-3; quote on p. 4-1.

81. Kornblut, 2005, p. 4-3.

82. Province, 1983, p. 27.

83. Province, 1983, p. 32.

84. Province, 1983, p. 32.

85. Province, 1983, p. 37.

86. Brands, 1999.

87. G. R. Shell, *Bargaining for Advantage: Negotiation Strategies for Reasonable People,* New York: Penguin, 2000, pp. 60–61.

88. Brands, 1999, pp. 62–63.

89. R. Fisher and W. Ury, *Getting to Yes.* Boston: Houghton Mifflin, 1981.

90. H. Mendelson and A. Korin, "The Computer Industry: A Brief History." Available online: http://faculty-gsb .stanford.edu/mendelson/computer _history/. Access date: Oct. 29, 2005.

91. Quoted in Safire and Safir, 1991, p. 31.

92. J. Pfeffer, *Managing with Power: Politics and Influence in Organizations,* Boston: Harvard Business School Press, 1992.

93. B. Morris, "The Accidental CEO," *Fortune,* June 9, 2003; quote on first page of article. Available online: http://www.fortune.com/fortune/ceo/articles/0,15114,457272,00.html. Access date: Oct. 31, 2005.

94. Morris, 2003, second page.

95. A. Bianco and P. L. Moore, "Xerox: The Downfall: The Inside Story of the Management Fiasco at Xerox," *Business Week,* March 5, 2001; quote on first page of article. Available online: http://www.businessweek.com/2001/01_10/b3722001.htm. Access date: Oct. 31, 2005.

96. A. Z. Kronzek and E. Kronzek, *The Sorcerer's Companion: A Guide to the Magical World of Harry Potter,* New York: Broadway, 2004, p. 394.

97. D.L.L. O'Keefe, *Stolen Lightning: The Social Theory of Magic,* New York: Continuum, 1982.

98. S. Larsen and R. Larsen, *Joseph Campbell: A Fire in the Mind,* Rochester, Vt.: Inner Traditions, 2002, p. 523.

99. Larsen and Larsen, 2002, p. 400.

100. T. Kidder, *Mountains Within Mountains: The Quest of Dr. Paul*

Farmer, a Man Who Would Cure the World, New York: Random House, 2004.

101. B. S. Peterson, *Blue Streak: Inside JetBlue, the Upstart That Rocked an Industry,* New York: Portfolio, 2004, p. 33.

102. Peterson, 2004, p. 40.

103. Peterson, 2004, p. 59.

104. Peterson, 2004, p. 90.

105. Peterson, 2004, p. 171.

106. Peterson, 2004, p. 238.

107. Peterson, 2004, p. 144.

108. Peterson, 2004, p. 145.

109. Peterson, 2004, p. 166.

110. N. Brodsky, "Street Smarts: Learning from JetBlue," *Inc.,* March 2004, p. 59. Available online: http://www.inc.com/magazine/20040301/nbrodsky.html. Access date: Oct. 31, 2005.

111. Brodsky, 2004.

112. D. Chopra, *The Way of the Wizard: Twenty Spiritual Lessons for Creating the Life You Want,* New York: Harmony, 1995, p. 3.

113. M. Ruhlman, *The Soul of a Chef: The Journey Toward Perfection,* New York: Penguin, 2001.

114. Chopra, 1995, p. 129.

115. Ruhlman, 2001, p. 268.

116. Ruhlman, 2001, p. 313.

117. Ruhlman, 2001, p. 282.

118. Ruhlman, 2001, p. 285.

119. Ruhlman, 2001, pp. 296, 310.

120. Ruhlman, 2001, p. 303.

121. Ruhlman, 2001, p. 303.

122. Chopra, 1995, p. 6.

123. K. Eichenwald, *Conspiracy of Fools: A True Story,* New York: Broadway, 2005, pp. 11–12.

124. B. McLean and P. Elkind, *The Smartest Guys in the Room: The Amazing Rise and Scandalous Fall of Enron,* New York: Portfolio, 2003, pp. 24–25.

125. Eichenwald, 2005, p. 2.

126. Eichenwald, 2005, p. 11.

127. J. C. Collins and J. I. Porras, *Built to Last: Successful Habits of Visionary Companies,* New York: HarperBusiness, 1994; J. P. Kotter and J. L. Heskett, *Corporate Culture and Performance,* New York: Free Press, 1992.

128. Eichenwald, 2005, p. 137.

129. Eichenwald, 2005, p. 633.

130. McLean and Elkind, 2003, p. 357.

131. Eichenwald, 2005, p. 11.

132. Burrows, 2003, p. 14.

133. Burrows, 2003, p. 120.

134. Burrows, 2003, p. 130.

135. Burrows, 2003, p. 124.

136. Burrows, 2003, p. 131.

137. Burrows, 2003, p. 163.

138. Burrows, 2003, p. 146.

139. McLean and Elkind, 2003, p. 134.

140. McLean and Elkind, 2003, p. 136.

141. Eichenwald, 2005, p. 72.

142. McLean and Elkind, 2003, p. 140.

143. Eichenwald, 2005, pp. 142–143.

144. Eichenwald, 2005, p. 144.

145. Eichenwald, 2005, pp. 270–271.

146. Eichenwald, 2005, p. 279.

147. Eichenwald, 2005, p. 387.

148. Kool-Aid got a bad rap. The drink used at Jonestown was a knockoff known as Flavor-Aid.

149. Ontario Consultants on Religious Tolerance, "The People's Temple, Led by James Warren (Jim) Jones," Apr. 4, 2003. Available online:

http://www.religioustolerance.org/dc_j
ones.htm. Access date: Nov. 30, 2005.

150. Kathleen Kinsolving and Tom
Kinsolving, "Madman in Our Midst:
Jim Jones and the California Coverup,"
1998. Available online: http://www.
freedomofmind.com/resourcecenter/
groups/p/peoplestemple/madman.htm.
Access date: Nov. 30, 2005.

151. Kinsolving and Kinsolving, 1998.

152. Dolbee, S., "Survivors' Perspectives
Differ," *San Diego Union Tribune*,
November 16, 2003. Available online:
http://www.religionnewsblog.com/504
8-Survivors__perspectives_differ.html.
Access date: Nov. 30, 2005.

153. Dolbee, 2003.

154. M. Popper, *Hypnotic Leadership:
Leaders, Followers, and the Loss of Self*,
Westport, Conn.: Praeger, 2001, p. 9.

155. McLean and Elkind, 2003, p. 142.

156. McLean and Elkind, 2003, p. 351.

157. C. Lindholm, *Charisma*, 2002,
p. 153. Available online: http://www.
bu.edu/uni/faculty/lindholm_charisma/
charisma.pdf. Access date: Nov. 30,
2005.

158. Lindholm, 2002, p. 163.

159. M. K. Ash, *Miracles Happen: The
Life and Timeless Principles of the
Founder of Mary Kay Inc.*, New York:
Harper, 2003, pp. 19–20.

160. H. Schultz, *Pour Your Heart into It:
How Starbucks Built a Company One
Cup at a Time*, New York: Hyperion,
1999, p. 14.

161. Schultz, 1999, p. 26.

162. Schultz, 1999, p. 101.

163. Schultz, 1999, p. 8.

164. Schultz, 1999, p. 331.

165. L. F. Baum, *The Wonderful Wizard
of Oz: 100th Anniversary Edition*, New
York: HarperCollins, 2000, p. 189.

166. From Wikipedia: Wisdom. Available online: http://en.wikipedia.org/
wiki/Wisdom. Access date: Nov. 1, 2005.

167. J. W. Meeker, "Wisdom and
Wilderness," *Landscape*, 1981, *25*(1).
Available online: http://phoenix.
isn.net/info/meekart.html. Access date:
Nov. 30, 2005.

168. R. A. Heifetz and M. Linsky,
*Leadership on the Line: Staying Alive
Through the Dangers of Leadership*,
Boston: Harvard Business School Press,
2002, p. 53.

169. J. Ortiz y Pino, "Whatever Happened to Wisdom," n.d. Available
online: http://phoenix.isn.net/info/
wisdompg.html. Access date: Nov. 30,
2005.

170. K. Freiberg and J. Freiberg, *Nuts:
Southwest Airlines' Crazy Recipe for Busi-
ness and Personal Success*, New York:
Broadway, 1998, p. 132.

171. J. Moyne and C. Barks, *Open
Secret: Versions of Rumi*, Boston: Shamb-
hala, 1984, p. 37.

172. The Wisdom Page, Review of
"Wisdom, Intuition and Ethics," by
T. Curnow, n.d. Available online:
http://phoenix.isn.net/info/wisdompg.
html. Access date: Nov. 30, 2005.

173. Personal communication to
authors.

174. O'Keefe, p. 142.

175. S. K. Langer, *Philosophy in a New
Key: A Study in the Symbolism of Reason*,

Rite, and Art, Cambridge, Mass.: Harvard University Press, 1958, pp. 39, 122.

176. Burrows, 2003, p. 56.

177. Baum, 2000, p. 170.

178. J. Campbell, *A Joseph Campbell Companion: Reflections on the Art of Living,* New York: HarperPerennial, 1995, p. 24.

179. H. Kelleher, audiotaped internal communication to Southwest Airlines employees.

180. M. Fox, *The Reinvention of Work: A New Vision of Livelihood for Our Time,* San Francisco: HarperSanFrancisco, 1995, pp. 1–2.

181. A number of investigations have reached similar conclusions. Examples include T. J. Peters and R. H. Waterman, *In Search of Excellence,* New York: HarperCollins, 1982, as well as Kotter and Heskett, 1992, and Collins and Porras, 1997.

182. R. Spector and D. McCarthy, *The Nordstrom Way: The Inside Story of America's #1 Service Company,* New York: Wiley, 1995, pp. 15–16.

183. Author's personal experience.

184. Fox, 1995, pp. 262–263.

185. A. Cohen, *The Perfect Store: Inside eBay,* Boston: Back Bay Books, 2003, p. 39.

186. Cohen, 2003, p. 167.

187. Personal communication to authors.

188. I. Broughton, *Hangar Talk: Interviews with Flyers 1920s to 1990s,* Cheney, WA: Eastern Washington University Press, 1988, p. 131.

189. C. Roush, *Inside Home Depot,* New York: McGraw-Hill, 1999, pp. 45–46.

190. N. Mokuau and J. Matsuoka, "Turbulence Among a Native People: Social Work Practice with Hawaiians," *Social Work,* 1995, *40*(4), 465–472; quote on p. 468. Personal communication with Keola Lake, Kahuna Nui, informed our discussion of historical developments in Hawai'i.

191. M. A. Meyer, K. Lake, and L. Altieri, "Ho'oku'ikahi: To Unify as One." Unpublished videotape, n.d.

192. Personal communication to authors.

193. C. A. Hammerschlag, *The Theft of the Spirit,* New York: Simon & Schuster, 1993, p. 50.

194. Valvano Foundation, "Jimmy V: Don't Give Up! A Tribute to Jim Valvano." Videotape, 1994.

195. B. Lopez, *Crow and Weasel,* New York: North Point Press, 1990, p. 1.

196. Author's personal experience. Terry Deal was standing next to the soldier when his daughter jumped into his arms

197. J. P. Mass, "The Kamakura Bufu," in M. B. Jansen, *Warrior Rule in Japan,* Cambridge, England: Cambridge University Press, 1995, pp. 1–43.

198. K. F. Friday, *Samurai, Warfare and the State in Early Medieval Japan,* New York: Routledge, 2004; S. K. Hayes, *Ninja and Their Secret Fighting Art,* Boston: Tuttle, 1990; S. Turnbull, *Ninja AD 1460–1650,* Oxford, England: Osprey, 2003.

199. Turnbull, 2003.

200. Sun Tzu, 2002 [500 BCE].

201. J. Leech, *Asymmetries of Conflict: War Without Death,* London: Routledge, 2002, p. 93.

202. Ambrose, 1970, p. 401.

203. Ambrose, 1970, p. 401.

204. Mao Tse-tung, 2000, p. 46.

205. Clausewitz, 1989 [1833], p. 276.

206. J. Moore and W. Slater, *Bush's Brain: How Karl Rove Made George W. Bush Presidential,* New York: Wiley, 2003.

207. S. Alinsky, *Rules for Radicals,* New York: Vintage Books, 1989; originally published in 1971.

208. Brands, 1999, pp. 120–121.

209. Brands, 1999, p. 122.

210. Brands, 1999, p. 124.

211. Brands, 1999, p. 125.

212. Brands, 1999, p. 125.

213. K. Maney, *The Maverick and His Machine: Thomas Watson, Sr. and the Making of IBM,* New York: Wiley, 2003, p. 437.

214. Maney, 2003, p. 137.

215. Maney, 2003, p. 242.

216. R. Worth, "What Lou Gerstner Could Teach Bill Clinton: Lessons for government from IBM's dramatic turn-around," *Washington Monthly,* Sept. 1999. Available online: http://www.washingtonmonthly.com/features/1999/9909.worth.ibm.html. Access date: Nov. 30, 2005.

217. L. Gerstner, *Who Says Elephants Can't Dance? Inside IBM's Historic Turnaround,* New York: HarperCollins, 2002, p. 198

218. Gerstner, 2002, p. 188.

219. Gerstner, 2002, p. 72.

220. Gerstner, 2002, p. 182.

221. Gerstner, 2002, p. 279.

222. L. DiCarlo, "How Lou Gerstner Got IBM to Dance," *Forbes,* Nov. 2002. Available online: http://www.forbes.com/2002/11/11/cx_ld_1112gerstner.html. Access date: Nov. 2, 2005.

223. R. Pernoud and M. V. Clin, *Joan of Arc: Her Story,* New York: St. Martin's Griffin, 1998, p. xiii.

224. Trial of Nullification Minutes. Paris, 1455. Available online: http://www.stjoan-center.com/Trials/null03.html. Access date: Nov. 2, 2005.

225. G. Chastellain, "Chronique des choses de mon temps [Chronicle of the events of my time]," cited in Pernoud and Clin, 1998, p. 167.

226. Pernoud and Clin, 1998, p. 159.

227. R. Caratini, *Jeanne D'Arc: De Domrémy à Orléans et du bûcher à la légende* [Joan of Arc: From Domrémy to Orléans, and from execution to legend], Paris: Archipel, 1999.

228. Caratini, 1999, p. 102.

229. Pernoud and Clin, 1998, pp. 17–18.

230. Pernoud and Clin, 1998, p. 21.

231. Pernoud and Clin, 1998, 22–23.

232. Pernoud and Clin, 1998, p. 23.

233. Pernoud and Clin, 1998, p. 28.

234. Pernoud and Clin, 1998, p. 29.

235. Pernoud and Clin, 1998, p. 10.

236. Caratini, 1999, p. 166.

237. Caratini, 1999, pp. 181–182.

238. Pernoud and Clin, 1998, p. 66.

239. Pernoud and Clin, 1998, p. 107.

240. Pernoud and Clin, 1998, pp. 111–112.

241. Pernoud and Clin, 1998, p. 116. Mandrake is a root often believed to have various magical powers.

242. Pernoud and Clin, 1998, p. 120.

243. Pernoud and Clin, 1998, p. 164.

244. Pernoud and Clin, p. 111

245. According to Roger Caratini, she was suffocated by smoke before the flames reached her body, and would have died "softly in murmuring more than crying the name of Jesus." Caratini, 1999, p. 329.

246. Pernoud and Clin, 1998, p. 136.

247. P. Mirvis, K. Ayas, and G. Roth, *To the Desert and Back: The Story of One of the Most Dramatic Business Transformations on Record,* San Francisco: Jossey-Bass: 2003.

248. Mirvis, Ayas, and Roth, 2003, p. 7.

249. Mirvis, Ayas, and Roth, 2003, p. 13.

250. Mirvis, Ayas, and Roth, 2003, p. 11.

251. Mirvis, Ayas, and Roth, 2003, p. 32.

252. Mirvis, Ayas, and Roth, 2003, p. 31.

253. Mirvis, Ayas, and Roth, 2003, p. 36.

254. Mirvis, Ayas, and Roth, 2003, p. 47.

255. Mirvis, Ayas, and Roth, 2003, p. 48.

256. Mirvis, Ayas, and Roth, 2003, p. 74.

257. Mirvis, Ayas, and Roth, 2003, p. 76.

258. Mirvis, Ayas, and Roth, 2003, p. 77.

259. Mirvis, Ayas, and Roth, 2003, p. 77.

260. Mirvis, Ayas, and Roth, 2003, p. 93.

261. P. Mirvis, personal communication, cited in Bolman and Deal, 2001, pp. 219–220.

262. T. Branch, *Parting the Waters: America in the King Years, 1954–63,* New York: Simon & Schuster, 1988. We have relied heavily on Taylor Branch's excellent and thorough account of King and his times. Other major sources included King's autobiography (C. Carson, Ed., *The Autobiography of Martin Luther King,* Los Angeles: Warner, 2001) and the Martin Luther King Papers Project (available online: http://www.stanford.edu/group/King/; access date: Nov. 2, 2005).

263. Branch, 1988, p. 119.

264. Branch, 1988, p. 139.

265. Branch, 1988, p. 166.

266. K. Andrews and M. Biggs, "The Dynamics of Protest Diffusion: The 1960 Sit-In Movement in the American South," Sociology Working Papers, Paper Number 2002-07, Department of Sociology, Oxford University, 2002. Available online: http://www.sociology.ox.ac.uk/swps/2002-07.pdf. Access date: Nov. 2, 2005.

267. Branch, 1988, p. 276.

268. Carson, 2001, p. 174.

269. Carson, 2001. p. 183.

270. "Birmingham Campaign," King Encyclopedia, Martin Luther King Papers Project, n.d. Available online: http://www.stanford.edu/group/King/about_king/encyclopedia/birmingham_campaign.htm. Access date: Nov. 2, 2005.

271. There are many sources for the text of King's address at the March on Washington, though not all record accurately what he actually said. One that does is on the Stanford University King Papers site at http://www.stanford.edu/group/King/publications/speeches/address_at_march_on_washington.pdf. Access date: Nov. 2, 2005.

272. J. Rotblat, "Einstein the Pacifist Warrior." *Bulletin of the Atomic Scientists,* 1979, *35*(3), pp. 21–26. Available online: http://www.thebulletin.org/pdf/rotblat/035_003_009.pdf. Access date: Nov. 30, 2005.

273. Brands, 1999, p. 299.

274. Brands, 1999, p. 212.

275. Brands, 1999, p. 211.

276. W. Whitman, "Passage to India," in M. Van Doren (Ed.), *The Portable Walt Whitman*, New York: Penguin, 1973, p. 284.

277. Brands, 1999, p. 151.

278. Brands, 1999, p. 145.

279. J. Klein, *The Natural: The Misunderstood Presidency of Bill Clinton*, New York: Random House, 2002, p. 148.

280. Klein, 2002, p. 148.

281. Klein, 2002.

ACKNOWLEDGMENTS

The older we get, the more aid we need, and we've been blessed with many friends and colleagues who helped make this book possible. First and foremost, we thank our friends at Jossey-Bass and particularly our supportive and tireless editor, Kathe Sweeney. We're grateful for Kathe's enthusiasm for the project, her many helpful ideas and suggestions, and her wonderful editorial input. Her remarkable ability to stay patient and cheerful even as our completion date endlessly receded is one of many reasons she is the worthy and beloved godparent of our effort.

The students in Lee's Fall 2005 leadership courses at the Bloch School of Business and Public Administration, University of Missouri-Kansas City, were enormously helpful in providing feedback and data that helped us improve the Leadership Images survey that appears in Chapter Two. The delightful and provocative members of PRIMA (Public Radio in Mid-America) who attended their 2005 conference in Kansas City also provided generous assistance on the instrument. The Brookline Group—Dave Brown, Tim Hall, Todd Jick, Adam Kahane, Bill Kahn, Phil Mirvis, and Barry Oshry—continues to provide vital professional and personal learning and support. Phil also provided helpful input in connection with his wonderful book *To the Desert and Back*, which we use in Chapter Nineteen.

Lee is grateful for the support and friendship of all his Bloch School colleagues—with a special nod to Nancy Day, Doranne

Hudson, and Dick Heimovics—and to his dean, Homer Erekson, who (among other contributions) approved the sabbatical leave without which this book might still be stuck in the pipeline. One of the best things that happened for Lee in the last decade was Bruce Kay's signing on as his administrative assistant. Bruce's reliability, steady good cheer, and continued willingness to do whatever it takes have been a huge help. Lee continues to be grateful to Henry and Marion Bloch for all their friendship and support.

As a result of his new status as a *retired* professor, Terry now fraternizes much less with academics and much more with his colleagues in the Edna Ranch Vintners Guild. His new colleagues rightly focus less on theories about leadership and organizations, and more on the process of winemaking: brix, yeast, malolactic fermentation, potassium metabisulfate, corks, glass, and, above all, sampling the fruits of their labor from time to time. Don and Priscilla Beadle, Jim and Jamie DeJong, Led and Ann Fortini, Ron and Jan Haynes, and Joel and Karen Schnackenberg form an awesome group of wine wizards. From time to time, individual members also respond to calls for advice on bookmaking. Vintners Rich and Sharon Pescatore experienced transitions at Hewlett-Packard and contributed thoughtful editorial suggestions on the present manuscript.

Bob Palmer, another Edna Ranch dweller, also contributed to the book's ideas through his fusion of modern medical knowledge with Native American wisdom. His insights from his Ojibwe heritage pushed us to expand our symbolic horizons.

From his hilltop home in North Carolina, Roy Williams offered valuable input from the works of Carl Jung. Keola Lake, now officially Hawaii's Kahuna Nui, was a deep reservoir of experiences, detailing how the Hawaiians are reclaiming the cultural heritage and identity that was wrested from them in the 1800s. As head of Hawaiian traditions, Keola exemplifies the wizardry that can transform human society.

We continue to learn from our children (we seem to have produced more wizards than warriors). Thanks again to seven very special people—Janie Deal, Edward Bolman, Shelley Woodberry, Lori Holwegner, Scott Bolman, Christopher Bolman, and Bradley Bolman.

In our first joint effort more than twenty years ago, we wrote to our spouses, "Thanks, and we love you." Remarkably, given the vicissitudes of modern marriage, they're still with us, and our love has deepened over the years. They generously continue to offer more love, tolerance, and sustenance than we deserve. Sandy performed far beyond the call of matrimony as the Florence Nightingale of San Luis Obispo, helping Terry transcend the assorted health hurdles that waylaid him during the writing. Aging has its costs. Sandy also provided a clinical psychologist's perspective on our efforts. Joan provided her usual combination of love, support, helpful suggestions, and unvarnished honesty in critiquing our work in progress. Her detailed commentary on the manuscript were invaluable. She continues to be a wonderful colleague and Lee's best friend. To Joan and Sandy, thanks again, and we love you more than ever.

THE AUTHORS

LEE G. BOLMAN is an author, teacher, consultant, and speaker who currently holds the Marion Bloch/Missouri Chair in Leadership at the University of Missouri-Kansas City.

Bolman has written numerous books on leadership and organizations with coauthor Terry Deal, including the best-sellers *Leading with Soul: An Uncommon Journey of Spirit* (1995, 2001) and *Reframing Organizations: Artistry, Choice, and Leadership* (1991, 1997, 2003). Other books include *Reframing the Path to School Leadership* (2002), *Escape from Cluelessness: A Guide for the Organizationally Challenged* (2000), *Becoming a Teacher Leader* (1994), and *Modern Approaches to Understanding and Managing Organizations* (1984).

He holds a B.A. in history and a Ph.D. in organizational behavior from Yale University. Prior to assuming his current position, he taught for more than twenty years at Harvard University, where he also served as director of the National Center for Educational Leadership and the Harvard School Leadership Academy, as well as chair of the Institute for Educational Management.

He lives in Kansas City, Missouri, with his wife, Joan Gallos, the two youngest of his six children, Christopher and Bradley, and an orthopedically challenged Dalmatian, Vincent Van Gogh of KCMO.

TERRENCE E. DEAL is retired from the Rossier School, University of Southern California, where he served as the Irving R. Melbo Clinical Professor. Before joining USC, he served on the faculties of the Stanford University Graduate School of Education, the Harvard Graduate School of Education, and Vanderbilt University's Peabody College of

Education. He received his B.A. degree (1961) from LaVerne College in history, his M.A. degree (1966) from California State University at Los Angeles in educational administration, and his Ph.D. degree (1972) from Stanford University in education and sociology. Deal has been a policeman, public school teacher, high school principal, and district office administrator. His primary research interests are in organizational symbolism and change. He is the author of more than thirty books. In addition to his work with Bolman, these include the best-seller *Corporate Cultures* (with A. A. Kennedy, 1982) and *Shaping School Culture* (with K. Peterson, 1999). He is a consultant to business, health care, military, educational, and religious organizations both domestically and abroad. He lectures widely and teaches in a number of executive development programs.

Deal lives on a vineyard in San Luis Obispo with his wife, Sandy, and their cat, Max. His current avocation is wine making.

Bolman and Deal first met in 1976 when they were assigned to coteach a course on organizations in the same Harvard University classroom. Trained in different disciplines on opposite coasts, they disagreed on almost everything. It was the beginning of a challenging but very prolific partnership. Their books have been translated into more than twelve languages for readers in Asia, Europe, and Latin America.

For five years, Bolman and Deal also codirected the National Center for Educational Leadership, a research consortium of Harvard, Vanderbilt, and the University of Chicago.

The authors appreciate hearing from readers and welcome comments, questions, suggestions, or accounts of experiences that bear on the ideas in the book. Stories of success, failure, or puzzlement are all welcome. Readers can contact the authors at the following addresses:

Lee Bolman
Bloch School—UMKC
5100 Rockhill Road
Kansas City MO 64112
bolman@allmail.net

Terry Deal
6625 Via Piedra
San Luis Obispo CA 93401
sucha@slocoast.net

INDEX